The deeply moving true story of giving up a life of luxury in a single irresistible moment

Sister Agatha
with Richard Newman

Published by Metro Books
an imprint of John Blake Publishing Ltd
3 Bramber Court, 2 Bramber Road,
London W14 9PB, England

www.johnblakebooks.com

www.facebook.com/johnblakebooks
twitter.com/jblakebooks

First published in paperback in 2017

ISBN: 978 1 78606251 2

British Library Cataloguing-in-Publication Data:

A catalogue record for this book is available from the British Library.

Design by www.envydesign.co.uk

Printed in Great Britain by CPI Group (UK) Ltd

3 5 7 9 10 8 6 4

Papers used by John Blake Publishing are natural, recyclable products made from wood grown in sustainable forests. The manufacturing processes conform to the environmental regulations of the country of origin.

Contents

PART TWO – POVERTY, CHASTITY AND OBEDIENCE

PART THREE – LIFE IS A PARADOX

Acknowledgements

Lady Victoria Getty, Mrs Biddy Chittenden, and the nuns of The Bar Convent, who have all been very good to me in answering my many questions with total openness when it was required.

Also, and especially, the help received from Sister Frances Orchard, C.J., whose expertise and knowledge allowed me to understand the complexities of convent life and gave me access to her world.

Most of all I want to thank 'Ag' – Sister Agatha Leach, C.J. – for becoming a very good friend.

Nothing is more practical than
finding God, than
falling in love in a quite absolute, final way.

What you are in love with,
what seizes your imagination,
will affect everything.

It will decide
what will get you out of bed in the morning,
what you will do in the evenings,
how you will spend your weekends,
what you read, whom you know
what breaks your heart,
and what amazes you with joy and gratitude.

Fall in love,
stay in love,
And it will decide everything.

Pedro Arrupe, S.J. (1907–91)

Preface

'I cannot remember a time when I wasn't in love.'

Agatha leaned towards me as we sat beneath the shade of a tree in the convent garden, a slight smile playing on her lips as if to tease me. Then, much more seriously, for she needed me to understand, she added: 'I've changed my mind on how I want you to begin. I want this book to start off the story as follows, then you can do the rest.' She proceeded to recite the piece in one run, clear in what she wanted to say.

'Will you tell me the way to Sligo? Because I wouldn't start from here. Now, I've always felt that if I was God, I wouldn't start with me. I know that God loves and cares for me, but He called me to be a nun and I would not have started with the person, or the background that I came from, when my other Sisters came from Catholic families, but, extraordinarily, He is with me… so this is my story told my way.'

Having set the bar she resettled herself in her chair and glanced around at the visitors arriving for afternoon tea in the peaceful garden, open to the public. Agatha is an intelligent woman, with over thirty years in this convent alone, and totally familiar with every operation that has taken place within the clutch of elegant Georgian buildings that form The Bar Convent, gently nudging the outer walls of Micklegate in York for 300 years. She exudes warmth towards the twenty nuns and other staff, which flow back and forth along the corridors as does the tide on a Cornish beach.

'My first idea was a bit too sensational, too tabloid newspaper and all that sort of thing, even if it was true – and it is – but this is a story, a very personal one, about God and me.'

This is indeed a story about a life in two complete parts yet each inextricably bound to the other by the same beliefs, constant threads in a long life. The first half is about Shirley Leach, the obverse side of Agatha, who retains the same mind, the same intellect, yet whose life is diametrically opposed to the younger version. On the one hand it tells of a young girl growing up in a twenty-three-bedroom mansion on the North Downs of Kent, cossetted and enjoying a 'glorious life' of dances, parties and flirtations; of horses and cucumber sandwiches on the tennis courts, with a butler in attendance to meet her every whim. Then there's the nanny, the governesses and her own groom. How does this fit when, in 1952, she received a message of such power and clarity that she wept for a day, raging at God for taking her life, and her fiancé, yet soon afterwards she was to change her name to Agatha and leave all that had once been precious to her folded away in a case?

PREFACE

For all the agnosticism of today, the disbelief and the downright mocking, one can be easily awed at her unbroken authority in the belief that caused her to surrender a life of luxury for a disciplined and meticulous Order, and at her sheer mental strength that few would be able to match even if they wanted to, certainly in the twenty-first century of self-indulgence and egocentrism.

It's not as though Agatha fits the standard image of the pious, silent nun, the projection on a wall of the good woman devoted to prayer and reflection. At least not on the surface, for she is as different to this as chalk is to cheese, or for that matter, whisky to Coca-Cola. She strides rather than walks through the building to meet me in the hall of The Bar Convent, the oldest unenclosed order in the UK, with the continuous presence of sisters since 1686. She has no habit or cap and veil to form an obstacle between us. Her beliefs are as strong now as when she received the call sixty-five years earlier and this conviction tells with every word she utters.

Her stories, her whole life, bubble out of her, unstoppable; each sentence is laced with humour, stitching in and out of her words like fine worsted cloth with, always, a mischievous glint in her eye. She is constantly astounded that anyone would wish to know about her.

Only once or twice have we strayed into a dark place (my description) when I raise the subject of 'that day' again. This was the day, an 'any sort of a day', a happy day, when she wrote to her fiancé telling him of the chairs she had found, and 'wouldn't they be just right for the new dining room?' Her hand had come to rest on the notepaper before continuing as if by itself – '*but I see no point now, for I am to become a nun.*'

There is a greyness in her eyes, like early cataracts, and I know that that apocalyptic event is as vivid and vital as it has always been.

Life, despite the security of the convent and her Sisters around her, has not always been easy, and when she became the Local Superior that period coincided with the threat of bankruptcy and loss of their home. Strength and belief allowed her to help redress the balance and how she achieved this is an extraordinary tale in itself. From this harrowing time she moved into calmer, if deeper, waters to develop her credo of 'Life is a Paradox'.

Whatever your beliefs, whether you hold any sort of theory on life after death, or even if you do not, this is a story that cannot fail to uplift you. This is the story of the life of Agatha, who, having been tested to the very core of her conviction, came out the other side, her faith secure.

After completing the first interview I asked what she would like to see as the main thrust of the book. Her reply was quick and unshakeable in her belief: 'God's dealing with me, we must lose a life to gain one.'

Richard Newman
Summer 2016

PART ONE

PRIVILEGE, PARTIES AND PONIES

1

Wakenings

It had been a sunny afternoon, one where the sunlight had poured into my room and onto my desk. It was so bright I had to shield the paper so I could read my words. There had been six dining chairs in an auction room, which would be ideal for our new life together, for we had plans to entertain quite a bit after we were married, and I was writing to my future husband so that he could decide whether I should bid for them. Excited, gloriously happy and secure in my future chosen life, I had always wanted to be married and to have children. Now I was going to do just that. My right hand came to a stop as I considered what else I needed to say and then, I began to write again: '*...for I am to become a nun.*'

There could never have been a clearer message than the one that stared out from the pale-blue notepaper in front of

me. I should not have been surprised – there had always been a feeling, a mood, some sensation that I was not alone, that God had something in mind for me. The comforts of my life had suppressed this emotional state of mind until now, in that sunny room. It was as if I had removed a pair of sunglasses on a gloomy day and seen, for the first time, my new world in sharp perspective. And I found myself saying, in the midst of weeping, one day I will wish I had said yes with courtesy rather than in floods of tears.

*

If my mother, Ximena, had had her way, I might well have been christened Hollyhock. If so, I would have been related to that other family of *Althaea rosea* (the very tall plant with pink or red cotton wool attached) rather than *Leach*, my father's name, of course, and Shirley Leach was a good deal safer. From time to time Mother did have some strange ideas, and Hollyhock was not even a Christian name, almost *de rigueur* in those days when a vicar might well ask a parent to include a John or a Matthew for the Church's sake. Besides, imagine the bullying at school.

Agatha arrived when I became a nun and derives from the ancient Greek meaning 'good', a fact I'm sure my mother was unaware of, or would have agreed with at the time, certainly not after a few years of attempting to bring me up in a noisy family. These days Agatha is undoubtedly out of fashion (all maiden aunts were labelled as such at the beginning of the last century, or so it seemed to me). At the time of writing the appellation is now ranked last in a list of 1,000 girls' names, which, maybe, is a

record in its own way. The original rise in popularity was created by St Agatha of Sicily, who was tortured on account of her beliefs in AD 251, which tends to stiffen my backbone if ever I'm asked the origin of my name. (The fifteen-year-old Agatha had the temerity to reject the advances of a Roman Prefect, resulting in her being tortured and condemned to death. A fortuitious earthquake provided a stay of execution but she died in prison.)

I only just made the dockside in Dover – I mean, literally, when the P&O steamship bringing our family back to England in 1931 from India included Mother at full term. Clearly I'd been waiting for dry land before my plaintiff cry was first heard, possibly on the basis I wanted a full British passport. My three sisters had all been born in Simla, holding *British Indian Passports – Indian Empire* on theirs. '*Indian*' meant the mighty State of India, but all the same, Great Britain did have a better ring about it and, remember, this was before the Second World War when Britannia still ruled some mighty waves.

From an early age I was, I sensed, a most unwelcome retirement gift. I had arrived some eight years after the youngest of my sisters, Pammy, at a time when my parents had far more urgent things to consider. Surely, in this case, three girls would have been quite sufficient? But having no son and heir can cause much anguish in some fathers' breasts, hopeful for the perpetuation of a dynasty to continue on command. Father had certainly tried valiantly, for Mother lost three other children on the way. Nonetheless, on 9 July 1931, I became the tail end of the family as Diana, we called her Didi (*Di-dee*), headed me by sixteen years, Lizzie followed by fifteen years, and Pammy by eight. Mummy was a beautiful

woman of forty, the most beautiful of us all, and my father was fifty-five.

Daddy had been summarily dismissed from his position as director of mines in India, where he had been based in Calcutta, having spent twenty years rising up through the ranks. As he had done so, he had attached three daughters in turn to the Leach household, with all the attendant comforts of servants which only members of the British Raj and the English aristocracy could truly appreciate.

The reason for our sudden departure after so many years was due to Daddy's firmness and belief in his knowledge of the mining industry. He had refused to give way to the British Raj after he had warned them in 1930 of an impending disaster in the Khas Jharia coal mine north-west of Calcutta – 'imminent' was how he described the situation. Khas Jharia was an enormous mine, hugely important to the economy, and those in charge flatly refused to listen to his warnings. As a result he was sacked from his job and therefore Mother, with me inside her blissfully unaware, and my three other sisters were placed on a P&O steamship bound for England. It was a shocking disgrace, yet, at the same time, it reflected the ideals of all that was then British – the stiff-upper-lip syndrome, a hangover of the great Victorian Age – and the two ideals could not be brought together in an acceptable compromise.

Back in Khas Jharia the miners continued to cut around the columns holding up the vast cavern to the extent that very soon after our family departed the roof collapsed, falling by eighteen feet. The mine was directly under the town and the coal caught

fire; if you pass by there today, you will see it is still burning, some eighty-six years later.

Seven hundred people were killed in that appalling disaster, including the man who replaced my father, but by then it was too late. I don't think Daddy was ever exonerated, as rightfully he should have been, and anyway he died within a very few years. Cleared perhaps but without a job, he was considered too much of an embarrassment to the mandarins in London. With few financial assets to support his growing family and the Great Depression grinding the soul out of Britain, he was cast adrift. The future could not have been more uncertain for the Leaches.

Years later, a vicar at Woodnesborough, near Sandwich, down in east Kent, told me he knew of a widow who had had a husband running a mine in India. He had been killed in a terrible accident. In a strange twist of fate it turned out to be the same man, the one who replaced my father.

The ease of life which my sisters and mother had always enjoyed was to cause them considerable heartache on returning to Britain. The year 1931 was a difficult time for them, re-adjusting to a completely new way of life, but utterly desperate for a large proportion of the population. Who were we to complain when there was starvation on the streets of this great nation? The very word, 'depression', summed up the mood on our arrival at the grey Dover dock, where a mournful fog accentuated the bleakness of life.

Almost as the great ship was tying up to its dock, my mother was rushed to the Grace Dieu maternity home in Dover, where

I was delivered with five of everything but without finding out whether it was day or night. I became a real being when my given name was affixed firmly to me: Shirley… Shirley Leach. There is a distinct possibility this was due to the currency of films in the thirties starring Shirley Temple and though the name was not one I myself would have chosen, there were hundreds worse. I have Daddy to thank for preventing 'Hollyhock' from being written in purple ink on my pink birth certificate. In modern jargon this would have been a bridge too far. As a first name, Hollyhock is rare, in fact it is less known than Agatha and derives from Holy Mallow, the common or garden weed. Thankfully, it was never more than a fanciful idea from Mummy. This was one of the times when Daddy put his foot down quite firmly: I was not to become a holy weed.

My arrival on this planet coincided with a number of fairly dramatic events. These included the advent of the Highway Code (would you believe it is eighty-five years young?). The Abbey Road Studios were opened by Sir Edward Elgar, conducting the London Symphony Orchestra playing 'Land of Hope and Glory', and the Royal Navy went through its mutiny at Invergordon in the September. There was also the opening of Whipsnade Zoo to Fellows of the Zoological Society and the general public two weeks before. Tremors from the Dogger Bank earthquake in the North Sea were felt all over the UK. The magic that is Google tells me it was a magnitude 6.1 for those who understand such things, the largest recorded earthquake in the country. Naturally, the greatest effects were felt on the north-east coast, though even in London *The Times* newspaper mentioned the fact that Doctor

Crippen's gruesome waxwork head fell to the floor of Madame Tussaud's emporium.

All in all, it was a busy year for me, notwithstanding that I spent most of it in my pram, looking out on the evolving world. Naturally I did not believe these portents were specifically directed towards me personally so I was happy to sleep through it all. More in focus with my father's point of view came the news that Winston Churchill had resigned from Stanley Baldwin's Shadow Cabinet, having disagreed with his policy of conciliation with Indian Nationalism.

This had been my father's daily world as he watched the rise of the Indian Independence movement which curtain-raised Mahatma Gandhi's civil disobedience crusade. Father must have surely felt the same misgivings as he furrowed his brow, directing it towards the insignificant figure of a man in a loincloth who swayed the minds of an entire sub-continent. Churchill had felt the same. One has to put this in its context of the time. Britain ruled the waves; we had three levels of class in this country, and the Indians had many levels of caste in their system. Gandhi, though revered today, was looked on in a very different light in 1930.

As soon as Mummy was strong enough – in those days mothers were expected to lie pale and wan for ten long days while they recovered (oh, how things have changed!) – we were eventually collected and driven to Temple Ewell, a small village not far from Dover, with a nice Domesday Book feel about it. Swerford, our house, had five bedrooms – quite large in today's ideal, but small for four growing daughters, each needing their own space.

Nanny arrived as a result of Mummy contracting puerperal

fever (a uterine infection) early on in my life, a not unknown condition of women having given birth, and she needed peace and quiet while she recovered. Pammy and I shared Nanny, removing the daily difficulties of nappies for me and keeping us clean out of Mummy's life completely. For the middle classes it was the accepted norm and underlined one's position in life. Nanny took our family name, Nanny Leach.

Compounding these events was the Great Depression, which sat upon everything else like a London smog. Daddy must have been worried, being without a job, crudely and cruelly set aside from the government with whom he had worked most of his life, like an empty salt cellar on a dining room table. Being a loyal British subject, he had asked if he should return to Britain at the outbreak of the First World War, but the government advised he would have more value remaining in India overseeing Afghanistan. He had wanted to be a vicar, the first in the family to hold an interest in entering the Church (that is, of course, the Church of England), and to support his beliefs he even carried in his pocket *The Imitation of Christ*, a devotional handbook written by Thomas à Kempis in the fifteenth century.

This, understandably, would not have brought in sufficient income to raise a large family. It took another four years of worry, of which I was wholly unaware, and I can only imagine the enormous gulf which had opened up as a result between his life at that time and the many years spent in India as director of mines. Out in Calcutta his position in society had been extremely important, ruled as everyone was by the Order of Precedence of which he was well up the list. He had known a time when women

would rather have pulled out of an evening's entertainment than not be permitted to enter the banquet or dinner at their rightful place on the list. Every person in this extraordinary world of the British Raj, from the Governor-General down to the lowliest cadet, was well aware of his fixed location in the firmament, and George Leach had been a rising star. The fall was hard and devastating in its effects, a crisis impossible to comprehend today.

So, with Mummy out of the loop for the time being, it was considered necessary that I have a nanny permanently. My first four years at Swerford with her by my side came and went in a series of increasingly strong flickering lights, the sort that catch your eye as you drive down a country lane past a hedge in low sunlight. Gradually the illumination grew stronger and longer as my memory improved and the fissures in my brain began to close up. There was the impact of parents, my sisters – who appeared so grown up, almost adults, to me – food and love. I grew plumpish and was labelled somewhat inexplicably by my nanny's mother 'My Little Apple Blossom' as I sat in my pram, studying this new domain of mine. By the time we came to leave the village, in 1935, I was fully aware of my family with its noise and bustle, though I had no idea of the straitened circumstances caused by Daddy's dismissal from the Service.

We left Swerford because of one of those fortunes of life when the sun came up very early one day and the scales at last tipped in favour of my parents. Almost overnight their worries vanished, or, perhaps it might be better to say three seconds after they opened the telegram. Mummy's father, Grandfather Hargraves, a successful solicitor and millionaire, had died, leaving his fortune

to his three daughters. Grandfather was, quite literally, our saviour. Young though I was, I remember him having a skullcap, which he always wore. He looked very Jewish, though in fact he was a strong Christian. His wife, my granny Ximena (like my mother), was nicknamed 'Perfie' by everyone who knew her, as she was considered perfect. Meanwhile, her husband courted his mistress, a woman named Ruby. However, for us the Hargraves camp was a date-filled oasis as life for my family was reversed in the blink of an eye. Daddy was able to buy Sibton Park set in the heart of the beautiful North Downs of Kent for the princely sum of £6,000. That is about £300,000 in today's money, a paltry figure for twenty-three bedrooms and forty-three acres, but the Great Depression was still running out of control through the country estates, their desperate owners often wiped out by the economic downturn of the Stock Exchange crash of 1929. As such, our house was acquired for a fraction of its real value. It was the time to buy if you had money, and that is what my father had – in bagfuls – and so he moved quickly.

*

At this moment in time I must admit the Leach family was extremely fortunate: God had smiled down on us. Along with my siblings and Mummy, I was removed to our wonderful new home at Sibton Park. Its finely clipped yew trees had been shaped into fantastical forms, the bountiful orchard was heavy with fruit, huge flower beds fascinated us, there was warmth in the colour of the weathered Grade II listed brickwork and forty-three acres in which to play and grow up. It was as distant from the Depression

as the far side of the moon, as if our small part of England had become its own island, with my pony to ride, trees to climb and the ritual of dressing for dinner as natural to me as my sisters had found it in India. Sibton Park became my home and I adored it – I wanted to live there forever.

For each positive in life there always has to be a counter-balancing adverse issue and it came out of Mother's good fortune. Father's family in Chesterfield, Derbyshire, of which there were thirteen, felt it would be nice if they were to share in our newfound wealth. Pressures mounted and in the end Father had to ring fence his family and specify all contact was to be through his bank. Over time, and with a general softening of attitude, he later relented and some of the family did indeed come to stay at Sibton, but the whole episode reminded me that arguments about money are always the worst, much as civil wars are always the most cruel.

Today, Sibton Park is a Holiday Property Bond complex, having previously been a rather smart school. I see that former pupils still correspond via Facebook, on the whole happy with their time at an establishment with a good reputation in a magnificent setting. Now it comprises forty-one properties: the Manor House itself was converted into thirteen apartments, and a further twenty-eight cottages and studios in the buildings surrounding the Queen Anne mansion boast, in Estate Agent speak: '…a large Reception area, a library, snooker room, and a Tudor oak-panelled long room and forty-one suites.' And, it goes on: 'a swimming pool [naturally], tennis [of course], bowling green [really?], a nine-hole pitch and putt…' The

hyperbole in the brochure continues with highly coloured pictures for the 'upsell' – at least I believe that's what it's called. It looks rather like an article for the *National Geographic* magazine. But it is nevertheless a beautiful home, and I still remember those happy days.

It is extraordinary, in this day and age, that in the 1930s Sibton would support just one family and its staff, while now there are homes for thirteen households in the main house alone. Of course it only serves to highlight the enormous gulf between those who at that time had almost everything and anything they needed and those often without anything at all.

As the country slid into an abyss of unemployment and soup kitchens, queues and tears, this real suffering was further whetted by the warning signs of an approaching holocaust: a second World War in the space of twenty-one years.

*

It was into this world of wealth, privilege and licence and against an increasingly worrying background of Nazi ravings and threats that I grew up, indifferent and cocooned by Nanny. There was ignorance towards the fact my mother hated the new house, especially when Father died in just over a year from cancer of the bowel (in those days coyly given the euphemism 'cancer of the back'). His death was sudden and thus shocking to my sisters, but at least they were able to retain images of Daddy, stories to tell of their lives in India, with him always there in the background. He had been such a figurehead they would have looked up to him as a very safe haven to have known.

Mother was enraged that George, her husband (known to her simply as 'Jim'), had left her alone with a huge house and four daughters to care for, let alone the staff to manage. She burnt all of his photographs, so I did not even have a photo of him for my bedside.

This grief levelled against the man she had married and spent so many years with in India sharing his bed made me realise things must have gone wrong for them earlier in their life together. The stresses of being without a job at Swerford must surely have taken their toll and when the cancer struck, it was over within a year. Medicine had not reached the degree of success that it has today – cancer was such a big dread in people's lives, they just knew immediately it was a death certificate. Daddy took a year to die and most of this time he lay in his bed upstairs going through who knows what pain. I was oblivious to any of this, so much so that when I was allowed into his room to say hello, I thought all daddies, especially *my* daddy, lived in a bed.

It had to end. No longer able to cope but perhaps clutching at straws, Mummy arranged to have Daddy booked into a London hospital. There might perhaps have been the vague hope of a miraculous cure. As both went to catch a train to travel up to the London clinic, she gently reminded him there would be no need to buy a return ticket for himself. Such was the finality of the sickness.

At the time I was not told of his death. It never reached the quiet backwaters of my nursery and I only learned of this loss when my French governess said that Daddy was dead and wasn't coming back. Mummy was livid, having wanted to protect me

for as long as possible, but the damage was done: I was five years old.

After the long, dismal funeral the family migrated back in convoy to Sibton for sherry and cocktail food, where we stood about in the familiar rooms now dominated by black, a scene composed of mourning veils and black ties. Mr Lewis the vicar came over to pay his respects and shake hands with our little group of close family members, all wondering what to do or say. After the brave words and kind thoughts of a funeral, to leave the lofty surrounds of the church one is left with a numb sense of finality: it really is all over, he or she is not coming back. That particular soul has departed and there can no longer be a desperate hope they will return in a day or two after a mistake or a muddle at the undertakers. The vicar must surely have felt the same way for he nodded at us girls before turning to Mummy.

'I'm so sorry, Mrs Leach, for your loss. I've lost something too. I had a very nice pair of kid gloves when I went in. Now they are gone… lost.' He held up a pair of blue-veined hands to emphasise the fact. Mummy brightened for the first time in the day at his words.

'Of course, Mr Lewis. Darling, go and find the Vicar's gloves for him.'

I scuttled off on the search. For all of her enjoyment in life there were rules Mummy had been brought up with, rules that could not on any account be transgressed. We knew them; we did not cross them. And, when it came to manners, good old-fashioned ones, Mummy was a true-blue Victorian, always there

to help, always seeing others were looked after before any of the family. The vicar was no exception.

Out of this small incident the Leaches adopted the phrase: 'Well, Mrs Leach, you've had a sad loss and I have lost my gloves' whenever anything went wrong. It's strange how such an event has stuck with me all of my life.

The one reassuring thing, I suppose, which came out of Father's early death (he was only sixty-one) was our continuing financial security. Mummy was alone, and she would never forgive him for this, but she had four daughters to bring up. They were going to need good husbands. Life was to be busy for Didi, Lizzie and Pammy, but India had been a very good training ground for Ximena Leach. Over sixteen years in the heat and chaos of Calcutta had allowed her resolve to stiffen, throwing up a wall against all the obstacles that life had, and would, throw at her in the future. There was that late-Victorian mental attitude (she was born in 1885) which enabled her to fill the vacuum so recently vacated by her husband.

Mummy was never a cosy person to know. Always extremely upright, she declined to stoop to anything or anyone, physical or cerebral. After all, there were staff to pick things up if she had dropped something, and no one in her opinion was better than her, so there was no need to look up to anyone. Expressions such as '*pas convenable, darling*' (it is just not convenient at the moment) and '*après, darling*' (not in front of the guests) came with '*pas devant les enfants*' (not in front of the children, i.e. me) – and, if my ears continued to listen, she and my sisters would switch to Hindi, leaving me enraged and none the wiser.

Mother was once summed up by a friend who said: 'It was better to work for Ximena than to be a daughter', as Mummy always treated her staff with the utmost courtesy. She would, nonetheless, insist her children were to be addressed as 'Miss Diana' and 'Miss Elizabeth', 'Miss Pamela' and later 'Miss Shirley', though as I was called 'Darling' by everyone, no one knew my real name.

As we readjusted to a new life of all females, we were now a matriarchal society of five, though with a sprinkling of males in the staff we were able to escape the crippling effects of the continuing misery of the Depression. In the South there were signs of spring in the unemployment figures, but in the North there remained a deep freeze. Just as the British Government was about to announce better statistics, the unemployment rate rose again, cruelly cutting off hopes for the manufacturing North. Alongside all of this worry our newspapers became progressively more alarmist as they printed black-and-white photos of a little man with a silly moustache and a floppy lock of hair. He would hold enormous rallies where most of Germany, it seemed, held up a flaming torch or a red, black and white Nazi banner against a pacifist world of appeasement. The idea of another war, so soon after the war to end all wars (sorry about the cliché), was unthinkable.

When Marsh our chauffeur drove the family, but not me regretfully, to Salzburg, Austria, in the summer of 1936, they were shocked at how widespread the menace had become. They returned to Britain chastened and not a little fearful. A dirndl skirt was brought back for me – like the obligatory T-shirt of today – my only memory of the time.

For the time being we could lose ourselves in the glorious countryside, unsullied by motorways and pollution. One day, sitting on a wooden bench watching Pammy and Lizzie play tennis, I asked Didi how Mummy had met Daddy in the first place.

'When was the first time she saw him? Daddy, I mean,' I demanded somewhat breathlessly, a plump six-year-old's rather cheeky request. Didi made a space for herself and pushed me across as she considered the question: should she tell me? Mother being a dyed-in-the-wool Victorian would never speak of such things – it simply wasn't done. Didi nodded to herself, having made up her mind I was quite old enough to learn the truth.

'Was he a knight in shining armour? Did she know straight away?' Somehow it felt right to ask for I was growing up fast. Those were dreams of my own, perhaps fashioned from storybooks but very real to me.

'Well, darling...' (Everyone was a 'darling' to Didi.) 'Well, Mummy had been quite ill and it was decided to send her away for some good sea air. That is what doctors did in those days, fresh sea air and saltwater was supposed to cure almost everything. She was staying with Granny in a nice hotel in Eastbourne, on the water's edge, if I recall, and, returning from a walk along the Promenade one day, she saw a bowl of peaches in the lounge. Hungry after her walk, she asked the waiter if she might have one...'

Aghast, I burst in: 'She didn't marry the *waiter*, did she?'

We were now at Sibton, with standards and... and... everything.

'No, of course not, darling, and *please* don't interrupt.'

She paused, annoyingly, then: 'Well, if there are no more interruptions?'

I wriggled on the bench, determined not to butt in again – this was a good story.

Didi went on. 'The waiter said: "I'm sorry, Miss Hargraves, but they have just been purchased by a gentleman on leave from India."'

'Ahh,' I breathed out silently now, considerably mollified. It was the answer I needed to hear.

'The waiter pointed most discreetly towards a handsome man coming down the main staircase. "That's 'im there," he said.

'Daddy, in a nice fashionable suit, walked over to the bowl of peaches at which moment, *carpe diem.*'

'What's that mean, Didi?' Latin had not yet reached the second floor where my nursery was to be found, so I interrupted yet again.

'Seize the day, darling. So Mummy seized the day. It was then or never. So she walked up to him and asked him outright if she might have one of his delicious peaches.'

'She *didn't*?' I looked up, stunned at the sheer bravado of the occasion. Didi was so ruffled at the story herself, she pulled out her cigarette case and lit up.

'She certainly did.'

'What did Daddy say?' I demanded between mouthfuls of apple, my equivalent of a cigarette.

'He said: "I would be delighted, Mrs er…"

'"*Miss*," Mummy said, most clearly and firmly. "Miss Ellen Ximena Hargraves."

'"Xi-mena, now there is a fascinating name. Do you know where it comes from?"

'"I believe it originates from the story of El Cid. I spell it with an 'X' but it comes from the Spanish 'J', but please don't call me Mina as do some of my friends."

'Father interrupted Mummy at this moment. "Ah yes, Jimena Díaz. She had married Rodrigo Díaz, who later became El Cid."

'They both laughed. Two months later, they were on a steamship bound for Calcutta. Poor Mummy, she had no one with her at the wedding after they arrived and it was only Daddy's Indian friends who were there.'

I exhaled breathily. 'What a lovely story! I hope I meet someone like that.'

'Oh, well done, Pammy!' Mummy sitting a little away from us and out of earshot circled a headscarf in the air, acknowledging a particularly well-executed volley. My mother played tennis by serving underarm, which was not exactly how the game should be played but we didn't argue: it was simply the way it was.

She continued, having found an audience. 'Tennis will help you all get on in life. It's important you can play so you join in parties and bring your friends back here for an afternoon. You can get to know a man by the way he plays, how good a loser he will be, lots of things,' she concluded somewhat mysteriously, though even I could tell by her face she had no idea what 'lots of other things' were.

I pouted a bit – well, quite a bit, in fact. At this moment I was not in the picture, there wasn't even an 'x' in my name. As she rose, Didi gave me a squeeze, a subtle reminder to keep the

secret, still cool though she had been sitting in the sun for some time. Whatever the weather she always managed to remain calm, a demure look on her face, in control of herself. She was, quite simply, superb.

*

My eldest sister was very special in my eyes and I adored her, not least because I knew she had magical powers harvested from her life in India. She had learned a secret Hindu poem by heart in which she was able to cast out devils from cows, a frequent occurrence when in Calcutta, I had learned, shaking with excitement, my mouth agape. Didi, like my other two sisters, had been born in the hills of Simla, where it was cooler than the baking streets of the city 1,800 miles away, and they had all picked up the language with considerable ease. She did manage to upset the professional fakirs, some bitterly complaining they were losing income each time she dashed off the Hindu poem, and levelled incantations in her direction: 'Miss Didi, I am very, very unhappy.'

Didi was small, petite even, beautiful and vivacious. She had told me that the news of my arrival had reached her at finishing school, the Monkey Club in Sloane Street, during a history lesson: 'I was so embarrassed, I didn't know where to put myself,' she explained.

I was unimpressed by her recollection. There were far greater things to be embarrassed about in my opinion.

'Darling,' demanded Mummy, 'ask Wright to bring down a tray of iced lemonade, there's a dear. No, on second thoughts,

he's off this afternoon. We mustn't disturb him. Go and get it yourself from Cook. Thank you.'

This was a pleasurable chore because I had seen Richards, the stable boy, talking to Cook at the back door. I was definitely in love with Richards, being all of six years old going on six and a quarter. Any chance to see him, do a bit of flirting, was not to be missed. No doubt, as I look back on that time, he thought I was simply the plump girl (well, I'm being kind to myself), Miss Shirley from the big house who spent most of her time demanding he saddle up my pony Peggy, always when he was busy cleaning the stables, and lead her out carefully on a leading rein as she was liable to bite anyone in sight.

'Yes, Miss Shirley,' he would reply to my demands, though dragging his feet towards the job in hand. He almost certainly muttered under his breath: 'Yes, Miss Shirley, no, Miss Shirley, and three bloody bags full, Miss Shirley!'

After meeting Mrs Richards for the first time, the idea of marrying her son began to pale quite rapidly as I did not think she would make a very good mother-in-law. It was probably because I wanted to swoon every time Richards passed by that I allowed the post office lady, Miss Collins (who as the choir mistress would always be replete with mortar board) to place a basin on my head to cut my hair. Mummy would lean over, saying things like, 'Don't forget the tips of her ears,' at which point I would close my eyes in case she completed her threat to carry out the amputation (in those days we tended to believe what our parents said). Miss Collins managed to make me look like any Friar Tuck from some long-abandoned abbey in the

north of England, for my hair had always been very straight and it remained so.

Later in life, I felt there was nothing wrong with leading a monastic life, but in those days looks began to be important – especially with three fashion-conscious sisters around me.

I had to look good.

2

A Doll Called Jeremy

Miss Shirley was becoming spoilt, I realise now. In those days I would wear a bowler hat, which I used for riding, but it remained there, covering that very straight hair at breakfast. Then came the days in the summer when I needed to look reasonable in a swimming costume and would take every advantage of being invited to Jeremy Glyn's (the banker) house, which had a swimming pool. There, I would daub my legs with the latest tanning paint, which managed to make them look like two sticks of carrots, though on emerging from the water I was returned to a whiter shade of pale whereupon I would have to go through the whole exercise once more.

With outdoor pursuits completed I would return to the top floor of one of the wings of the house (why always the top floor? A bit like a Hollywood film, I fear) with Nanny, completely

separated from my two elder sisters, who each had a large room to themselves. I recall Lizzie's bedroom was called the Flamingo Room but my nursery was named 'the Nursery', disappointingly enough. My room was divided into the day nursery and the night nursery. Nanny and I shared the night nursery, and Pammy would keep Nanny company in the daytime along with me. As the evening drew on Mother might play me Chopin's *Berceuse* and I imagined the animals going into the ark two by two. It was a tranquil life, a world away from the cold, dark streets of children with rickets, the drawn eyes of hungry mothers and fathers queuing, anxious to be seen as they sought work in the docks and the building sites.

The world for me was created by Nanny, who was wall-to-wall fun. Each day she would take me out, sometimes delivered to the site by our chauffeur, where we might take a wind-up gramophone so I could listen to 'The Teddy Bears Picnic'. Summer days were idyllic, tempered only each evening when I was brought down to the drawing room for 'cuddly time', which I found simply loathsome as it meant a matinee tea-time on-stage performance in front of Mummy, my sisters and often a guest or two. Later, when future brothers-in-law began to appear at our house for afternoon tea, they would ask me if I 'had had my milkies yet?' Ugh!

There came the occasional win when Cook served one of our hot curries to potential new additions to the Leach family at smart luncheons, the recipes successfully transferred from India via Pammy's Ayah, and I would secretly chuckle behind my napkin as they choked on their chillies. I suppose, had I not been

angelic, I might have asked, 'Would you like a glass of milk to cool it down?'

There were, nonetheless, considerable disadvantages in being not only the youngest member of the family but, due to the yawning gap between even Pammy and myself with our eight years, let alone Didi's sixteen, I was seldom allowed to pry into the world of practically grown-up women.

To alleviate some of the frustrations I was given a series of dolls. For me nursery life meant dolls and one in particular I named Jeremy. It turned out to be an eerie insight into the future for, eventually, there were three Jeremys in my life – and all at the same time! For now, I want to tell you about the first, a china doll neatly dressed by Nanny, who had made him a smart red blazer and trousers. Jeremy was part of my life until I was nineteen years of age when I dropped him on a hard, unyielding floor and Jeremy Number One was no more.

As I stared woefully at the pink and white fragments, I suddenly realised, 'There goes my childhood.' It was as far as I could go. Awful as the tragedy was, there could be no tears: Mummy did not approve of them.

It was a strange name for a doll, even though Pammy's doll was called Michael and, more curiously, my first doll was Trixie Trufood. I have no idea why I called her after a 'nutritious cat food made with a blend of baked grains', but I must have liked the alliteration even in those days. What is more curious is to call any of my toys 'Jeremy' for we had no family connections with that name, yet within just a few years I would allow the name to touch my lips many times in a day. Jeremy Number

Three was, in fact (to give away a secret early in my story), to become the light of my life. Unknowingly, but perhaps the reason I named my doll as such, I had met a Jeremy Chittenden for tea one day at Sibton when Mummy invited his family over for the afternoon. Although it did not impact me then, it was a portent for the future.

Meanwhile, I learned to jump on my pony and kick a ball around the garden with a friend called John, who was to leave my playground for Eton. Together, we managed to create our own world in the gardens, which were kept immaculate whatever the weather. Our head gardener was known as Rudd, whom my sisters somewhat unkindly nicknamed 'The Udder', though one must assume, for decorum's sake, if nothing else, they did not say so to his face. Rudd had come from being a gardener at the Duc de Stacpoole's vast gardens. There was also an under gardener, though I have no further memories of him so perhaps there was no mutual attraction. Or, maybe he was always in the potting shed. Come to think of it, that was probably why Richards was not mutually attracted to me: he was always hiding in the stables, keeping out of my way.

On Nanny's half-day off my sisters were given the responsibility of looking after me, a task for them and a real trial as far as I was concerned. On her return each week Nanny would bring a small present back with her and would always ask the same question: 'Has she been good today?' It's surprising I did not like dangled carrots more than I did.

As sure as daylight rose each day the reply would, inevitably, be: 'No, she has been absolutely *ghastly*!' – a word frequently

used in those days and one often incorporating two As in the pronunciation. I would do my best to ignore the remarks and try at the same time to disregard the still-damp marks of what suspiciously might have once been soup stains down the new wallpaper.

Nanny would often bring me out to the garages, where we kept a Daimler. Alongside it was a Hudson Terraplane (I'm advised it was a 'straight eight'). Those two cars were the responsibility of the chauffeur, to whom Nanny would talk quite a bit – well, quite a lot, in fact – much of it in lowered tones and with considerable sideways glances at me. At the time I was too young to understand the reasons behind my pram being pushed into the yard of the garages to meet Marsh. It was not just for the fresh air: Nanny had fallen in love with our driver, shiny leather boots and all. One day they announced they were to be married and my whole life fell in like a row of dominoes, leaving me bereft.

All at once life wasn't quite as good as it had been. Marsh had proposed, Nanny had accepted, and I was precipitated on the back of their happiness into an enormous black hole. She had been around since forever, it seemed: my prop, my defender against the worst of my sisters' japes, and my constant companion. And she was able to answer every one of my 'Why's' as if she knew everything in the world, and her hand had always been there to cross the road to stroke a horse's nose or talk to a dog. It was thus impossible to imagine a world without Nanny.

Only much later in life did she come back to see me, well after Daddy died, at which point she let me know she considered him to have been a wonderful man. Like a drowning mariner, I clung

to those words for, without a photo of him and conversation muted whenever his name was raised, it was tough trying to place him in any sort of warm light.

While all this tumult was boiling up around me and the days slipping by quickly, with Daddy's face beginning to merge into a blurred blue horizon, I found it comforting, looking back, that God was often there beside me, or at least He seemed to be there, though I could never be quite sure who God was. At my age I felt He must be a big man, but I hadn't any clear vision of what He should look like although I decided He had to be a warm man, kind and gentle. I liked those thoughts. His image or presence was subliminal, dancing out of sight each time I tried to focus on his face, the sort of experience one gets with a swarm of midges on a fine summer's evening. During those years He might have been re-reading up on his earlier decision to make something of me. A few hums perhaps, a puzzled frown as he looked down on my latest escapade. He might even have encouraged my governesses in their attempts to teach me values I might find useful in convent life. The older I grew, the easier it became for me to refer to Him almost as if He was walking along beside me or sitting in the opposite chair, but for now I was quite content to have Him there as a comfortable new presence. Though too young to analyse it, I'm sure it never bothered me – it was just something I grew up with, like an iPad used by today's children. The fact He was there seemed quite natural for me to accept Him just as He was. Unlike most of the family, I could summon Him up without having to pray. Advantage, Shirley.

As Mother required me to read a chapter from the scriptures

every day it was easier to recognise, perhaps, that it formed a conduit linking my readings to my future life. I know today this was the very earliest intimation that this someone was going to be around for the rest of my life.

He was possibly surprised at my eternal badgering of my mother when I would ask her to let Bobby come to tea. I must quickly explain that Bobby was the previous owner of Sibton Park and after we moved in, he would stand out in the road, leaning moodily against the gate while he stared into the kitchen garden.

'Mummy, Mummy, can't we invite Mr Howard in for tea? He looks so lonely out there!' would be my regular plea.

'No, darling. We cannot.' Quite firmly. 'One day you will understand why I cannot agree to your request, but for the time being, no.'

Mystified, I would return to the attack, each time I saw him there. Parents can be *so* annoying at times.

'Mummy, Mummy, Mr Howard is there in the rain, getting soaking wet. *Can't* he come to tea?'

But it was no use. Only after I came of age, and thus could talk about the taboos we all lived under in those days, did I learn Bob was gay. Why this should have meant we couldn't have him round for tea remains a mystery. Gay, of course, was not a word in common parlance in the 1930s. There was 'fruitcake', and even earlier men might be described as 'artistic' and girls might be 'sporty', innuendoes which the whole world knew and understood, and translated into their real meaning. Their language went deep underground and took the tag 'Polari', in other words a means

of communicating to others of the same sex without Great Aunt Mabel becoming aware something was amiss.

All this was way above my head as I stared forlornly out at Bob through the rain-dappled windows. To an innocent young girl it was so unfair that he could not come and have a cup of tea and maybe some of Cook's Dundee cake. I realise now that Dundee was, in fact, made up of fruit, so perhaps not the most subtle of proposals.

Dear Cook... I was fascinated with Dorothy's ability to produce meals of all sizes and a range of exotic menus. There was something so exciting about a kitchen: its clunk of heavy pans. The roar of the blue gas flames licking the sides of an aluminium pot, the scent of curries and roasting beef were the precursors to my own lifelong interest and involvement in food. I had been told that Dorothy was cooking on gas and to my small mind that meant she lived on the top of one of those giant gasometers which used to dominate the skylines of towns. It conjured up this fairly reasonable picture, at least to me, of Dorothy actually having a house planted on the top of the steel dome. While walking with Nanny I would crane my small neck skywards and enquire: 'Can you see Dorothy on the top, Nanny?'

Alas, I never did see Cook's house on top of that gasholder.

Then, a big day in my memory, Jordan came to work as the groom. You will recall I had Richards placed at my sole disposal as a stable lad, a luxury in itself as none of my sisters rode. However, Jordan took over the running of the stables and in so doing taught me that hard work made one a better person. I

simply adored the man who told me to muck out the stables and clean the tack rather than leave it to the lad. Soon after he arrived he showed me how to toss fresh straw in the air towards the sides of the box to ensure it was soft for my horse when it lay down. It was my first true contact with the adult world and I began to worship the very ground he walked on.

Horses arrived one after the other, beginning with ponies and graduating up to bigger steeds as I grew and matured into a reasonably competent rider. My world became filled with stroking velvety noses and combing manes, the application of saddle soap, blacksmith visits with white hot heat on my face, and hunting, of course.

My first pony, Peggy, was horrid – a biter – though I soon moved up to Wendy, then Peter Pan, on to Whisky and finally Stardust. Where the name 'Whisky' came from, I have no idea as Mummy didn't drink and I was too young to make the connection to the colour of the drink. Come to think of it, it could have come from Jordan himself.

Jordan had retired from looking after a stable of horses whose exalted owner had jumped with them at Olympia, so naturally he wanted to see what I could do. Hating jumping, nonetheless I did as I was told and was schooled and, much later, properly trained up for racing in a point-to-point. Thankfully, at the last moment, my horse went lame and I was excused the agony of leaping over what looked like enormous fences, undoubtedly higher than me. It was thus quite useful when I learned to pray on a horse.

Let nothing disturb you, let nothing affright you…

…which was worthwhile saying and quite appropriate for the time. The horse seemed to like it as well.

Riding could bring me to a state of exhaustion. I had started at the age of six, yet often when I got home from a long day of riding I was too tired to sleep. As I lay on my bed, still smelling of hay, I would watch with growing horror as a witch with its broomstick moved up and down my curtains. Often frightened out of my wits I would call out the name of Jesus with no idea why, which miraculously calmed me and the witch would disappear. In the background, as if hovering over my head, I knew this was yet another instance of realising something or someone was watching over me, that perhaps it was this God I had been told about in church, who seemed to pop up wherever I was. It was a very difficult idea to follow at my young age, nor did it go away as I grew older.

So I moved through and up my birthdays in a strong Church-of-England atmosphere, strengthened by my mother's religious application to everything in our lives, and allied to this rather marvellous God of somewhat mystic origin suspended over me as he let His presence be known from time to time. Mummy, however, if she had been reading these words, would have reminded me to add, 'But tell them Low Church, darling: *Low Church.*' Anything that smacked of elitism was not for her and by association, not for me.

All this religion ensured the whole family at Sibton attended church each week, never missing a service whatever the weather. Going to church meant the whole family, dressed in our Sunday best, sisters' hats at a rakish angle as we walked together up the

road in line abreast, accompanied by the family Pekingese – the one that would later bite the soldiers when they moved into Sibton – chuckled at life to the extent we would hold up all the traffic, which was forced to remain at a crawl behind us until we passed into the churchyard. The Pekingese dog, whose name was Peke-Frean (after the Peek-Frean biscuit), did not enter the church, I'm fairly certain, so it must have remained outside. Once there, we sailed up to our Sibton reserved pew, studied carefully by the remainder of the congregation, but we didn't care: life was good. We even sat in front of the local doctor, unheard of in those days.

Didi, Lizzie and Pammy were growing up into lively young women, their ages now ranging from twenty-two down to thirteen, who enjoyed life to such an extent it could sometimes carry over to the church service itself. On arrival we would be quite breezy; Shirley naturally, if coyly, smiling at the choirboys. We would eye up the vicar as we counted the number of hymns on the board and call out 'Coo-ee!' to the curate, whose name really was Cooey, would you believe. It was all a ritual, led by Mummy, a task from which we could not escape, and as certain as the milk would be delivered on Monday. We were not permitted to shuffle or whisper, replacing these with demonstrations of our perfect manners, which we had had drummed into us over the years until they became automatic.

Then the mood would change to enrichment as we stood for the next hymn; Mummy had a habit of singing the wrong verse, but such was her dominance over us no one would utter a word. All we could do was bury our faces in handkerchiefs with muffled snorts of porcine revelry.

Being so much younger and solely because of my age, I was allowed home before the sermon began. This meant one of my sisters would accompany me, allowing the two of us, in summer, to get to the ripe peaches in the greenhouse before the others, duly moralised and sermonised by our ardent vicar, returned ready for lunch. Always there would be an 'It's my turn to take Shirley' argument as each sister recognised the value of (a) Missing the sermon, and (b) Gaining the advantage of having a riper peach than the others. There was thus a value in chaperoning me for I was not permitted in those days to go astray from the house or its grounds without a follower of some sort. Mummy was locked in an age before the Roaring Twenties, pre-First World War and Victorian in every respect. If we wanted to go out, we had to be accompanied by someone responsible. It was right and proper, the way things were 'done' in those days, and was not seen as anything out of the ordinary in any way for those with money.

With Nanny gone, when I was just six, came the end of the nursery and the start of a series of governesses to educate me in the ways of the world. The first one, a Frenchwoman, I did not like at all and I like to think she smelled of cooked garlic. Lessons were alleviated by breaks where I spent time with a boy called Bobby, with whom I got on well until one day he shut me in the drawer of a wardrobe, causing me to collapse into a blubbering wreck.

'That's not a very nice thing to do!' I sobbed.

But I did get my next pony from his family. Named Wendy, she began to show a marked interest in the stallion in the next field. Regrettably it was my cold, calculating nature which went

into high gear. No one was watching, so I opened the gate and allowed Wendy to trot gaily into next-door's field, whereupon the stallion became somewhat agitated. Hey presto, Wendy became pregnant! When the foal (Peter Pan) arrived, no one knew what had happened, so I trained it up to jump and sold what turned out to be a very nice pony for a hundred pounds, a considerable sum in those days.

*

Mummy was settling down to life without Daddy and had made the decision that mauve or purple were to be her colours in the future, making a real break from the past. She continued to wear those shades for the next forty years until her death. As time went on though, I began to feel that all had not been well in the months leading up to my father's death. Daddy had never disclosed if he had really wanted a son, but there had been many attempts, I feel sure, to retain the name of Leach. Then, quite clearly, Mummy had come to the conclusion that enough was enough, that there was never going to be a son for Jim, whatever they tried. I was to be the last in the line. And so she made the decision to stop having babies that could lead to miscarriages, which had been so painful, every one of them. She decided she ought to buy a contraceptive 'just in case', as it were.

One day, face set resolute, she marched into the chemist's shop and made straight for the counter before her nerve gave way. After stumbling with her words, which somehow did not want to come out of her mouth, she managed to make the girl understand her needs. Receiving a typical pre-war reaction in

the form of a withering stare, Mummy backed out of the shop, mortified, embarrassed – and with no protection.

*

While Sibton slumbered in the heat of that summer of 1936, history continued to lay down new deposits of rather more interesting events for us to read about and discuss over afternoon tea, apart from the usual death of a king, abdication of the next and installation of yet another, all in the same year. Though thought-provoking and of profitable glee for the newspapers, it was somehow paralleled by the opening of Billy Butlin's first holiday camp at Skegness and the introduction of the first speaking clock by the GPO. The dear girl who provided the time over those heavy black telephone handsets had an accent which could etch glass, but at least it was a start. I wondered what Daddy would have made of the tragedy at Wharncliffe Woodmoor colliery in South Yorkshire that summer when an underground explosion ripped through the coal face, killing fifty-eight miners. It would have set him thinking of what might have been in India had he been listened to, but he died a few months before the disaster. I'm sure had he lived he would have known in his mind he had done his duty, and it was not his fault he was discounted by the mess and tangle of the Civil Service.

And, as the first Supermarine Spitfire lifted into the air over Eastleigh Aerodrome on 5 March 1936, the country began its long but inevitable descent into war.

3

Early Days

Up to the time of the Declaration of War my world had been jam-jar filled with horses, rabbits (I was president of the Rabbit Club!), tennis and fun with Nanny despite her constant 'Elbows off the table, Darling!' Her departure meant the arrival of the aforementioned governess in the angular silhouette of Mlle Olive the French mistress (the garlicky one) and then Miss Kathleen, who travelled together by bus each day from Folkestone. They employed varying techniques to teach me, and six others, in the vicarage.

These governesses – both spinsters, they all seemed to be spinsters in those days – had been trained under the PNEU system, at the time a revolutionary scheme for teaching. The Parents' National Education Union was unique, created by Charlotte Mason, whose credo was to have short periods of learning of

twenty minutes each. This was bound to a philosophy of 'I am, I can, I ought, I will'. Children, she said, should be respected, and she dismissed as 'twaddle' materials that were dumbed down and insulting to them. Miles ahead of her contemporaries, her principles still hold strongly in the United States.

Meanwhile, we worked from nine in the morning to teatime, Monday to Friday, being picked up by the Vicar and having to ride behind him on his bicycle, something I hated. We had the weekends off when I reverted to my normal self in the gardens and the surrounding countryside.

Despite the short lessons, there were many of them as a result. I did daydream quite a lot – well, more than that – about my horses and rabbits. My mother was somewhat disappointed that I did not do better at Religious Instruction exams (R.I., as we called it then), but it did not seem to worry me at the time. When I challenged her, saying she had never had to take such an exam herself, she replied most firmly, 'Oh yes I did and I received ninety-two per cent.' She would never have used such phrases as 'I *got* ninety-two per cent' as I myself would probably have used in that context. To her the word 'got' simply did not exist.

Those exams were strange. Although I was only six or seven, I think, I could write quite nicely but I had to answer the questions verbally, dictating to my mother, who wrote the answers down, causing her to collapse from time to time in fits of hysterics into her lace handkerchief. Of course this did not improve my confidence, watching Mummy hooting into her hankie, but I also have no idea what she wrote down in response to my garbled replies. For all I know she may well have falsified the

answers. Whatever she did, those were then sent to Ambleside, headquarters of the PNEU, for marking, though, regrettably, I have no memory of receiving any results. Perhaps the only one was the result of the R.I. exam.

Laughter blended well with the occasional delight and one special delight dropped into my lap that summer. Lizzie was courting *heavily*, a word I rather enjoyed, and she was never around at that time to give me a hug. Eventually there came a day when Robert ('Bobby') Richard Patrick Spens called officially, asking to see my mother (there was, of course, no man for him to seek for Lizzie's hand). Mummy took him into the garden behind some yew trees while Lizzie sent me to spy on them, me being the smallest and the most cunning. I could feel my heart pounding away in my chest for the whole thing was like a dark thriller.

I arrived to overhear Bobby confirm he had had three mistresses. Now I presume he was confirming, in his own way, he was experienced in all matters of schooling, but I was not sure if he had related the story in the past perfect tense, I have to admit. I had missed the first, all-important bit and, anyway, I was not at all sure what this all meant for Lizzie. Let's face it, what was a mistress if not someone who taught you English syntax? Breathlessly, I scampered back to where my sisters stood in the house, hands clasped tightly together, as I reported the facts although, when challenged, I could not tell them whether the three mistresses were still on the scene, or had been one at a time, or all together, or had been long gone – fairly vital pieces of missing information, it must be admitted. I did, however, feel very important as joint spy and telegram girl.

'*Three*!' said Lizzie. 'Poor Mummy, she has had to handle the whole thing on her own. How naughty of Bobby!'

Whatever else was said, and I would have loved to have been a fly on the wall at the time, approval was given for the wedding to proceed but not until a suitable length of time had elapsed 'for decorum's sake' and 'to be sure, darling'.

It was the first of the promises Mummy kept in order to ensure her daughters married well. As Bobby's father, Sir William Spens, later became a senior judge in India (in fact the last British judge before the British withdrawal in 1947) he was considered to be a 'good catch' – as if he were a cleanly netted, six-pound rainbow trout.

Then came a morning, a Sunday, when we were all attending matins. It was, with hindsight, an event Ealing Studios later screened successfully, but here it was in real life. The south door opened as the service was in mid-flow and a man entered, removing his cap into his pocket before walking the entire length of the main aisle while his boots clattered on the tiled floor, exaggerated by the total silence of the congregation. At this point the music had died as the organist also followed the progress of the feet, all that were visible from the keyboard. This simply wasn't done even if it was Low Church. All heads had turned. Such an event had not happened before. We studied the progress of the well-dressed man towards the Vicar. There came much whispering in each other's ears before the Vicar stood back and thanked the man. Our Reverend cleared his throat and we knew it was something better than his usual announcements.

'Friends, I have something important to announce…' As he

gave a pause so that every member's eyes were upon him, he grew a little in height. 'Britain has declared war on Germany.'

It was Sunday, 3 September 1939.

Instantly there was consternation in the congregation. The chatter rose in volume, parishioners turned round, elbows draped over the pew backs, ignoring the Vicar, who was forced to pat the air in vain as he implored us all to pray for peace. I was eight years old and had neither images of the last war nor had I experienced the loss of a family member as so many had done. But there were plenty of people attending that day who had, and the usually peaceful sound of matins had taken on a distinctly sour note. The choir mistress, Miss Collins, still in her mortar board, struggled to retain harmony, but for today it was lost in the gloom, and left a discordant note hanging above our heads. It was sad, as she had one of the most beautiful choirs in the area, especially known for their rendition of 'O For the Wings of a Dove'.

The phoney war followed, a strange time where very little happened, and certainly did not fill up many pages in my diary. But there was one event which revitalised our day. We had occupied our time by cajoling the staff into digging an enormous hole ready for our air-raid shelter. When a cow fell in, surprised at this obstacle in its usual path on the way to milking, the whole scheme was abandoned and instead we decided to use the wine cellars. Why we didn't think of this at the beginning, I have no idea. Each time the sirens wound up into a yowl, we would go down the steps and sit among the Château bottled clarets and the aged ports while waiting for the All Clear. It was a curious place to wait out a part of the war,

the air filled with musty odours of long-spilt wine and pure age, not at all sure anyway if the ceiling above our heads would protect us should we receive a direct hit.

Winter came and went. Then came the marvel of Dunkirk, turning the phoniness into stark reality. The war had just become serious and brought fear or, if not that, considerable anxiety to Sibton. We were so close to the coast, our lanes became choked with trucks filled with exhausted soldiers too tired to smile, but at least they were safe and one day they would be ready to fight again.

Such a failure made the whole country sit up: we were about to be invaded. This manifested itself in the form of the London Rifle Brigade setting up an operational headquarters on our estate. The LRB, as we came to know it affectionately, had been formed out of the London Brigade and went on to commit brave wartime acts overseas. For the foreseeable future we would share our house with the Army.

Sibton was requisitioned for the war effort but, remarkably, my mother and I were permitted to remain in the house. Lizzie was now married and her husband Bobby was already at war so she joined the Auxiliary Territorial Service (ATS). Didi followed in the Women's Royal Naval Service (WRENS), while Pammy, not to be outdone, decided to join the First Aid Nursing Yeomanry (FANY). This reduced the Leach family to a total of two, with most of the staff already planning to leave, either because they were called up or had to work in a factory.

It was a time of enormous upheaval and no one quite knew what was to happen. Communications were slow, if non-existent,

confusing the otherwise precise tones of the BBC News, so it was also a bewildering time, to say the least. Bewilderment on the one hand but hard realisation on the other, as we understood only too clearly we could be occupied at any time from now on. Sibton was just a few miles from the invasion beaches that had proved ideal for the Romans, let alone William the Conqueror. The German barges had begun to amass on the other side of the water, waiting only for Hermann Goering's Luftwaffe to destroy our planes before setting out towards our own white cliffs. For all we knew, Sibton had already been selected as the headquarters for some high-ranking German general.

With the arrival of the Army came some reassurance. The soldiers were led by a brigadier, who came to live in the house. Tommy Fairfax-Ross, M.C. was the man to bring stability back to our small household. A major and a captain also stayed in the house and the rest of the Company occupied every bedroom available with the exception of Mummy's and mine, which had belonged to Pammy. No one else was permitted to call on us and the place was off-limits to everyone.

The bonus for me came in the form of the Brigadier's batman, with whom I fell in love on the first day. As the average was about seven hours he certainly fell into that category. Tommy's men were fully armed but there was no barbed wire round the house. It did mean, however, that each time I returned from a ride on my bicycle or pony, I had to give the password – almost as good as Arthur Ransome's *Swallows and Amazons*.

The ten loose boxes, one of which was used for my rabbits, were turned over for the Brigade's stores, but Wendy my pony

stayed out in the park most of the time and the most important thing was I could continue to ride.

So we settled down to the routine of a completely new way of life, accommodating the soldiers in the ground-floor rooms, with no restrictions on where we went. Much to my disappointment there was no sign of a secret map being covered up hurriedly as I approached, and no scenes of officers nodding in my direction, as if to say, 'Quiet, Sir, we are being overheard!' The only time we did not mix was for meals.

My mother befriended the Brigadier, a brave soldier from the First World War who had been awarded the Military Cross in 1917. Tommy, with his dapper moustache and Brylcreemed hair, swept back as was the fashion in those days, became a firm friend. I, with my newfound love, the batman, would creep upstairs, where I would help by putting two drops of 'Oh-my-bath' essence of oils in his bath, which in fact was my mother's bathroom, while my own private soldier kept cavey, a terrified look frozen permanently onto his features.

If you study any map of the south coast you will see how Sibton Park is very close to France, or 'occupied France' as we were now well aware. By 10 July 1940, the heat arrived with a glorious summer coinciding with the first waves of German bombers: the Blitz had begun. Almost without a break, battles were fought above our house as our men fought desperately to keep the bombers from reaching our shores. Riveted to the action 10,000 feet above our heads, the batman and I would climb out of Pammy's bedroom window onto the flat roof of the loggia, where I would watch the spiralling vapour trails

against the hard blue of the sky. Often, spiralling vapour meant a plane was falling to earth and a brave man of either side might be about to die.

One day, one of our pilots directly overhead must have been successful for a parachute floated down quite quickly into the Park, causing alarm to the soldiers, who dashed off with their bayonets flashing sharply in the sunlight, much to my delight and my mother's amazement. This was not an event which happened every day and never at as close quarters as we now experienced. Here was the war, upfront and personal.

The Messerschmitt pilot, for that is whom it turned out to be, had arrived for an early tea. I mean that literally for we were just serving up afternoon tea while enjoying some of Lizzie's wedding cake left over from the ceremony.

My face lit up. 'Mummy, can I take a big piece of cake to the pilot? They think we're starving and he will realise we're just as good as them.'

'Certainly, darling. Give him a nice slice.'

The astonished pilot clicked his heels and started to eat from a porcelain plate while his bemused guards shuffled uncomfortably in their boots, not at all sure if this was correct or proper. It was 'certainly not in the Army Regulations,' whispered one, then reddened as he realised he had been overheard. Neither the two of us nor the soldiers had taken in the fact that the men's loaded rifles and their very sharp bayonets were trained on us as we had been proffering cake to our enemy, in an ardent wish to see he understood we were not starving. Had the pilot suddenly shouted out 'Boo!' we, and the soldiers, would have been lying on the

ground with a dozen holes through our bodies. Almost certainly the pilot would have walked away, completely unscathed.

He was a good-looking lad, smelling of glycol and engine oil, and responded politely with '*Danke, danke, Fraulein, und danke, Frau*', addressed smartly to my mother, who gave him one of her winning smiles to make clear she was still the head of the family in this household despite the soldiers surrounding her with a ring of steel. I was surprised he did not attempt to kiss her hand and I'm sure had he done so Mummy would have accepted the offer graciously.

While he was searched, presumably for guns or poison pills, the soldiers took away his personal photographs of his family. I found this a shocking act and still do today. Unable to get through to headquarters, possibly due to the raid continuing, the pilot was locked in the green bedroom (or was it the blue one?) for the night and a meal sent up to him. I cannot recall if the house silver was used, or a damask napkin folded on the tray, but we received no complaints from upstairs. The next day he was driven away somewhere. Poor man! I always wondered if he managed to get his photos back to while away the long hours in the POW camp.

With both Didi and Lizzie married, and all three of my sisters now doing their bit in the Forces, Mother and I found ourselves alone with almost all of the staff now having departed for the Forces or factory work. We had kept one on as a general help and I seem to recall another girl from the village, who somehow managed to make us feel very unnerved. Throughout this time we were grateful for the comforting presence of Tommy Fairfax-Ross and his band of men, as shadows loomed larger when we were on

our own. The blackout in the corridors was darker without the familiarity of the continuous noise of past years to brighten the corners, as there had always been a member of the household to help out at the single press of a bell. The drear mood of the war advanced by the day until it seemed trapped in the very fabric of the walls. The house wasn't ours any more and I wondered if it would ever be returned to us so that it could recover the happiness locked within those very same rooms.

But, and here comes the rub, with Dorothy the cook gone, Mummy and I had to fend for ourselves and anyone else who wanted to chance food poisoning. In fact I owe my conversion and religious vocation to my mother's inability to make good gravy, a fact I will explain later on. By good gravy, I mean the brown stuff that coats the meat with a tasty covering that enhances the food and blends deliciously with mashed potatoes and Brussels sprouts rather than, as she managed, to kill the roast – *any* roast, in fact – with a thin grey gruel. I suppose, if I'm honest, neither Mummy nor I at this time had any idea how to cook anything at all. My sisters would have been no help anyway had they been permitted to turn up on a weekend leave with their husbands or boyfriends in reluctant tow; instead they had to chance a restaurant, where there was very little choice on the menu.

Our inabilities to master the works of Escoffier or Carême were all too clearly evident. It caused a blend of blood (sharp knives), sweat (hot kitchen), tears (many) and toil (without diminishment), which paralleled our magnificent Prime Minister's words exactly. It was as though he had spoken to us directly through the modern medium of the wireless straight into our house, er… kitchen.

The kitchen itself did not help us improve our skills. It was not a place, in those days, to hang about in as we do today in our shiny modern *cuisines*. The wartime galley was a fairly hideous place to work, with its scrubbed heavy-top pine table always needing cleaning, loaded with splinters, getting in the way of carrying hot dishes, while the stoneware sink was too low for our backs. It held a wire basket filled with leftover pieces of soap. This latter 'invention' was there to try and raise a froth, usually in vain, while doing the dishes. We found out, eventually, through a series of experiments that we had other cleaning aids to fall back on. There was Zebo to blacken the range and Silvo and Brasso (still found in supermarkets today). Oxydol sponsored the *Ma Perkins* radio show with its first laundry soap and as a result created the first soap opera (true). Pride of place at the back of the sink on a cracked white-tiled sill stood the Vim container. You can imagine the tears when Vim was first introduced to our manicured hands and nails. 'Red, raw, ragged and rough' is the phrase which comes easily to mind.

Before the onset of war, the cooker had been an enormous Esse heated with coke, which allowed the coal dust to settle at a rate sufficiently intense that in one day one could scribble one's Christian name on any surface in the room. This was eventually replaced by a sparkling gas cooker (which lived on the top of the gas holder), saving us many hours of cleaning. The one other useful piece of equipment we had purchased was the newly arrived refrigerator, standing on a set of curiously naked legs, which meant curdled milk, penicillin moulds and fish our dogs would regularly turn down were now things of the past – especially helpful with the summer of 1940 being one of the hottest of the century.

As the Battle of the Atlantic took its frightful toll on our convoys, food began to run out. We were introduced to ration books and stubby pencils, the latter to mark the former on arrival in the shop. For some curious reason these pencils, this time provided by the shopkeepers and accompanied by much licking of the lead (for what reason I still have no idea), were usually about one inch long. I never saw one any longer and pondered why the Government only issued a standard one-inch pencil. War savings, I can only deduce.

One egg, two ounces of butter and four ounces of bacon each week made it a very small meal on a plate. The upside was I began to shrink as my puppy fat gave way to a much more shapely silhouette. Food could not be wasted and we were forced to eat everything on our plates. To supplement these meagre rations, wild game, feathered and furred, were real finds, but on arrival in the kitchen we had no idea what to do with them, even if they resembled a still life painted by Breughel or van Aelst.

The problems began to build like cumulonimbus over a sunny beach in August. We had to skin, pluck, gut, chop and pare. Furthermore, we had to boil, broil, steam, stew, bake, baste, roast and fry. We scoured our hedges for rosehips and nettles, thus increasing the aggravation to our already Vim-reddened hands. In the autumn we picked hazelnuts, teased blackberries from their thorny stems, plucked mushrooms in dewy dawns and foreign fungi which, wisely, at the last moment we abandoned, as they didn't have that all-important furry ring on the stalk. We shaved butter into microscopically thin slices and divided sugar up as if it were cocaine with a piece of card

(credit cards had not yet been invented), but, oh, for a pair of Marigolds! They were not to come along until the fifties, invented by the J. Allen Rubber Company, and in those early days were orange rather than the characteristic yellow of today. Now, *that* is interesting, Agatha!

You would think that Mrs Beeton might have been much sought after, but her recipes were always on the basis of 'Take twelve eggs…' and we, no mathematicians (actually, we were hopeless at sums), had no idea how to reduce this formula down to one egg. For that matter we were pushed to know how to boil that single egg for breakfast.

Poor Mummy, I was no help at all – she was on her own. Most days, she would climb up into an Army truck to be driven to Folkestone to buy fish at McFisheries, not only for the two of us but the Rifle Brigade as well. I can only assume the soldiers had their own cook for we might otherwise have found ourselves in very hot water on a charge of having incapacitated an entire platoon in one meal. But my mother had survived the transition from being a British Raj's wife to a pretty good housekeeper in Kent and rose magnificently above the privations the Second World War threw at her. She became exceptionally good at entertaining the officers' wives at Sibton and at the end of the occupation by the Rifle Brigade they presented her with a silver box, an act which greatly touched her as she had not expected anything at all.

Christmas arrived. Another trial, associated as it is with gargantuan and varied menus. It became a trial of Herculean proportions as we tackled the turkey, or was it just a largish

chicken? I could see by the time it was ready to go into the oven the stuffing was about twice as large as the bird itself, perhaps burnt on one side and raw-ish on the other, with *that* gravy on top, but it brought us together, full of hope for an early Declaration of Peace.

On less festive days I rode around the hard tennis court in endless circles without using my hands to show off to the young, yawning soldiers. They had got used to me jumping out at them from a particularly dense bush, shouting '*Hände hoch!*' (Hands up!), which was a bit foolish as their rifles were loaded, the invasion imminent and nerves stretched to breaking point. Because of my continuing antics Mummy would, by urgent necessity, on approaching a sentry from behind, call out in a very clear accent, 'It's alright, Sentry dear, it's only Mrs Leach,' followed by a rather limp hand wave to catch the attention of a nervously distended pupil, which allowed time for its owner to ease forward the safety catch on their rifle.

Poor dears, I'm sure we didn't make the war any easier for them.

My dogs would often run beside my bicycle, barking their enjoyment. Most of the time Dawnie, Duskie and Blossie were quite placid animals, yet they managed to terrify the soldiers on guard, most of whom had been brought up with dogs as mangy strays in their streets or fierce guard hounds. Sometimes one of them would have to be sent to find me to remove the fourth dog, Peke-Frean the Peke, who had gone to sleep in the main drive, because an Army delivery was due. They assumed they would be automatically bitten, should they approach any of our dogs, though it was usually the Pekingese, about eight inches high,

who took the trouble to get up off its hind legs and administer a rather sharp, flesh-puncturing bite.

It was while we were coming to terms with the war rampaging out of control overseas, when we thought things were bad but not too awful, that the conflict came and touched us directly, shocking and sudden and so final. In 1942, we received news that Lizzie's husband, Bobby, had been killed at sea while a prisoner of the Italians. We presumed he had been captured in one of the great battles of the Western Desert and was being shipped back to Italy on a tramp POW steamer, the *Ariosto*, to wait out the war. The irony, we later learned, was that the ship had been torpedoed by a British Submarine, HMS *Upholder*, returning to base at the end of a successful mission against the Italian Navy. Our submarine unfortunately caused 160 men to be lost out of a total of 410, of which 135 were Allied prisoners.

Bobby had also been born in India, so there were strong links with our family and he had had almost no time with Lizzie after they were married. The one good thing arising out of the tears and grief was her daughter Helen, a healthy girl who had been born during the Blitz. My mother had insisted that Lizzie have her baby in London as she could not have it at home in Sibton – not the best decision when bombs were falling around them. Eventually they returned to their own home, glad to be away from the threat of the nightly raids. By the end of the long hot summer, the Luftwaffe had been reduced by a significant degree and Hitler turned his attentions elsewhere. With the immediate peril of invasion removed, Sibton was a much safer haven than the London Clinic.

As well as the personal hurt to the family, with its sudden silences and awkward moments as we realised Bobby was never coming home, it was also Britain's gloomiest hour: we retreated from almost everywhere. In February of 1942, Singapore, the diamond in the East, surrendered. Our Merchant Navy suffered appalling losses so there was a good chance we might be starved into submission. It was at this lowest point that Mummy made the courageous decision to send me away, not to a farm in the country for safe keeping, but to Miss Faunce's school in Shaftesbury, Dorset. This meant she would be alone in the house with the Army and she would have to feed my twelve rabbits and exercise my pony. Strict instructions were issued by me to ensure the rats were kept out of the hutches, as they were prone to eating the babies. Less babies, less income, I calculated, though Mummy felt a better description was more 'calculating'. 'Cunning' is the other word which comes to mind.

Miss Faunce had run a successful day school in Queen's Gate, London before the war, but the German bombers put paid to that. Lord Shaftesbury, in an extreme gesture of goodwill, handed his Dorset home of St Giles House at Wimborne St Giles over to Miss Faunce to continue her sterling work. It was a good arrangement for him as his granddaughter became a pupil at the school. They were kindness itself in handing over their home, with Lady Shaftesbury bringing us strawberries at night during the season. Once a term we were all invited to lunch with her and her husband – nice people.

With the house made available, Miss Faunce had moved lock, stock and barrel and added boarding facilities. Perhaps

unsurprisingly it was to be called Miss Faunce's School PNEU. As an interesting footnote for me, having a lifelong interest in food, Sir Antony Giles, who was briefly Elizabeth the First's Secretary for War, introduced the original cabbage into England from Holland.

Well, that *is* very interesting, Shirley!

From the very first day I found myself blissfully happy, enjoying the best time of my short life. I was eleven years old by then and for me the hardest part was being frequently frozen by a combination of a bitter winter and little heating. Getting into bed was agony, even with socks kept on all night to keep away the worst of the chilblains – a word you don't get to hear much of these days, with every house centrally heated.

Studying the names written in spidery ink on the back of the standard elongated school photos, everyone but me, it would appear, had some sort of link to royalty of British or European ancestry. To underline my own lowly position, their names were often double-barrelled as if this were de rigueur in declaring one's wealth and ancient lineage. It was a necessary appendage, as was a crystal-cut accent and beautifully coiffed hair. I came to the conclusion Shirley Leach, with her dead-straight locks, was really not in the same league.

There were forty-two of us and we were taught music by Miss Ennion, who automatically became 'Miss Onion', and Miss Strickland took art. There were others, each attempting to move us in the direction all nice girls were supposed to go in those days, with subjects which would be sufficient for most girls, who would be going on to secretarial courses or nursing. Women, or girls, were then expected to fill the more trivial jobs before

ending up as wives, sitting at home to look after their children. Careers were but for the few.

Having no exeats in wartime Britain meant we only came home for the holidays. It was difficult enough as it was, with little fuel to move around the country, so this was discouraged as much as possible. It left us with the main events such as Christmas and Easter. This meant arriving by train into Waterloo from Andover, where I was picked up by a driver as Mummy didn't drive. I often wondered if she, never having driven as there had always been a chauffeur for her, regretted not having learned, as the prescriptions of war changed everyone's habits.

On my return home for the holidays I was told I showed more interest in my rabbits than my mother, but this was almost certainly due to me becoming very nearly a teenager. There was much fluttering of wings on the edge of the nest. Also a need to have some time to myself after the intimacy of the boarding-school dorm. This manifested itself one day when I was combing my hair in my bedroom, while having to listen to my mother once again sounding off against my father. I had heard it all before but this time I hit her with the back of my hairbrush – not too hard, but a reminder I did not wish to hear it again. Daddy was gone; he wasn't coming back, and there was nothing anyone could do about it. We all missed him in our own way.

I realised Mummy was intensely lonely, more so after having sent me off to school, and this was the only reason for lashing out at Father, or anybody for that matter. This loneliness unfortunately clashed with my own awakenings, the parent attempting to hold onto the last of her four offspring, the other, the burgeoning

teenager, desperate to take flight. Beginning to assert myself, I wanted to be heard above the din and clamour of the war.

Apart from the cold at school, soap rationing had been introduced – yet another comfort item removed from our lives. Milk was reduced to two and a half pints a week at the same time. We began to notice how Britain was drawing in on itself as lives and treasure poured into the sands of Tobruk and the ice-cold green waters of the Atlantic. There seemed no end to the misery and the cut-backs, no light at the end of the tunnel. It made it difficult for me to learn to fly by myself, or to plan for the future.

Up in York the saying goes, 'There's now't as queer as folks' – which could be applied equally usefully down in Sibton. Below the froth and bubble Didi's husband, Geoffrey, was giving her a hard time. Although affectionately nicknamed 'pink and white' in his hunting colours – he was an amateur jockey – much to Didi's dismay he was becoming a hopeless alcoholic. The hurt could not have been greater or more painful. Though amoral in some ways, he could also be, by contrast, a very kind man. It led to confusion at times, but the iron grip of alcohol was claiming a member of our family and it would not be the last.

A distraction arrived in the form of squads of GIs, Yanks and Americans. They were everywhere in their distinct better-cut uniforms with their silk stockings – not for them, of course, but for us hopefuls – along with gum and cigarettes. There appeared to be a seemingly bottomless store of these goodies, which were distributed around the county at the many dances I was starting to attend whenever I was home.

Silk stockings were one thing, but a bottle of imported tomato ketchup proved too much for Mummy.

'What on earth is that?' she exclaimed to Didi and Lizzie, home on leave, as a bottle arrived on Didi's otherwise pristine table. Her finger, straight as an arrow, determined exactly what she was levelling her ire towards.

'It's all right, Mummy, we always have those on the tables in the NAAFI. It's nice to have with a cold pie, or some chips.'

I think she was winding our mother up, but it was water off a duck's back.

Mother replied with her customary firmness: 'It is *not* alright, *this* isn't the NAAFI!'

She clasped the bottle before dropping it like a dirty nappy on the sideboard, well away from her offended eye. We all smiled into our knees – good old Mummy!

It was the British, though, who were better at swearing than our American cousins, many of whom hailed from the Bible Belt and were unaccustomed to hearing Anglo-Saxon being spoken quite so openly. Emboldened, one day Lizzie uttered the word 'Bugger!' which instantly invoked Mummy's wrath, having overheard. She took us all to one side for a lecture: 'I never want to hear that word again.'

But Lizzie was none too concerned as she had a good store of other words saved up and we simply replaced that word with '*le bougé*', a word we conjured up five minutes after the edict. It was quite satisfying to me at eleven years of age to say that someone, quite close by even, was a little *bougé*. I knew it wasn't so naughty as the other word it had replaced and I still used it sparingly, like

ground cloves in cooked apples. It was never deployed in front of Mother in case she had the translation. On reflection, although the word was created on a whim, *la bougie* also means 'candle' in French, which somewhat lessens the impact of its usage, but as we were ignorant of the fact in those days it retained all its flavour of naughtiness.

The war might be raging around us but Christmas holidays meant, with my riding experience, I could be the whipper-in at the local hunt known as the East Kent Hunt and about as low-brow as you could find this side of a large fox hole. I continued to be ghastly, believing the Leaches to be above the motley huntsmen and girls. When I heard a rider talking of '*the* hounds', I would lean back in my saddle and turn to face the miscreant with a withering look: 'Hounds, hounds, Sir, never *the* hounds.'

I repeat, I was *ghastly* in those days.

But fox hunting was in my blood. Roaring over the fences, shouting to each other as we jumped, was great fun. It was a mob gone mad when we sighted a fox and the horses just took control, and it was easy to understand how a cavalry charge became an unstoppable event. I was quite close to the Master of Foxhounds, which I reduced, naturally, to MFH, though I needed to keep him at arm's length. He had once been invited to Sibton before the Army arrived and succeeded in pinching the bottom of Lizzie's lady's maid, who was filling in, serving dinner. It was hard enough for her to exclaim loudly and he was not asked again.

Hunting conjured up the equally pleasant smell of the damp woods when I went cubbing – the sort of smell that stays with you all your life to reignite old memories when next you inhale

that earthy odour of rotting logs and wet lichen mixed with pine gum and not least, of course, the instantly recognisable scent of the fox itself.

The Christmas of 1942 found us in unusual circumstances – at least, comparatively, when it came to buying presents, for there simply was nothing to buy in the shops. Mummy never missed, though; there was always something placed under the tree. In return, I kept her reasonably happy during that festive season by suggesting that when I came in from a dance I should pray on my knees for the time it took for a birthday candle to burn out on a dish.

Today, with memories not as clear as they once were, I try hard to think back to what we did at the time. Away from my friends at school we all had to resort to listening to *Much Binding in the Marsh* and *ITMA* every week, along with *The Brains Trust*, the latter to make us feel we were testing our intellects. Mother and I would rail at the wireless when we knew an answer before the team, though none too often, I recall. At the time radio, or rather 'wireless', was an enormous attraction. It was automatic to turn the set on and wait while the valves warmed up as soon as I arrived back in the house.

Along with almost everyone in Britain, Mummy would always listen to the news, her head leaning across the wireless speaker as if that made it more clear, for those were days of continuing worry. Britain's fortunes on the front rose and fell in line with the tide at Bristol Docks, but we did end that horrid year with the announcement in the usual clear and calm notes of John Snagge at the BBC, of Rommel's final retreat from El Alamein.

As we listened to Winston Churchill's glorious speech, 'This is not the end...', Sibton rejoiced, and I became aware of abnormal, different stirrings in my mind. Each time I tried to retain them, like a gnat over my head they would appear tantalisingly for a moment, yet each time I grasped at the annoying midge, it would disappear round the back of my head to stir the same memory once again. There was a mood about me that was not just about filling out physically, but a new mental awareness of something special in the air. I had no idea what it meant, nor was there any reason to care especially, except when alone with my thoughts.

Out riding on my own on a beautiful morning, with the dew soaking my pony's fetlocks, there would come a feeling of such excitement I would flush in anticipation of something hidden just round the next hedge perhaps, or someone stopping me on my horse to say, 'Life is going to get very much better.' I put it down to growing pains, and so did my sisters, and the close contact I had with their husbands; they all believed my own Mr Right was round the next corner.

Looking back, it was remarkable just how long we persevered in holding onto our established way of life – standards, Shirley, *standards* – in this egalitarian age. It would be very difficult to make one's grandchildren even begin to understand why we did so, but it was all part of the war effort. In our tiny, bloody-minded way, repeated thousands of times over the country, none of us were going to allow the Hun to alter our way of life for one second. As a consequence we changed for dinner each night (which I did on my own, as my lady's maid had long gone), even when dinner, 'supper', as we call it today, consisted of macaroni cheese and

stewed apple. It was expected; we weren't going to give way to the Nazi blitzkrieg as we shook out the spotless linen on the table and arranged damask napkins in flutes or bishop's mitres.

On top of these privations we had to endure doodlebugs, which my horse hated and which made it difficult to catch and calm her as they droned low over the park. This was followed by the V2, but we never saw or heard these nasty rockets for they were travelling at 3,500 miles an hour, too fast for anything let alone the bat of an eyelid, and the first anyone in London was aware of was when there was a huge explosion.

At the end of all the horror, the needlessly spilt blood and the dreadful decimation of families, the people rightly danced in the streets and scaled lamp-posts to wave their flags. Pammy, the sister closest to me in age and the last of the three to wed, married a Pole. He was Stephen Dyboski, a Catholic no less, so the marriage was solemnised in a Catholic church in Spanish Place, London, surrounded by the destruction the war had brought. Massive raking shores held up the ends of torn buildings, propping up dreams of a better future, while children rode up and down the muddy slopes created by the bomb craters in soap-box carts, oblivious to the cost in human lives and much of our national wealth.

Stephen had met Pammy while she was serving in Italy in the FANYs and he was one of those incredibly brave men who organised parachute drops of ammunition, medicine and food behind enemy lines for the Warsaw Uprising of 1944 in support of the partisan groups. He was a brilliant man, having quickly escaped from Paris where he was at school to join the Free Polish Army; he was also an outstanding musician and a linguist.

Mummy, on learning of the budding romance far away, demanded Pammy return home, which she did, unescorted through wartorn Europe only to arrive to be greeted by our mother's well-remembered phrase: 'You are very welcome, darling, but I'm afraid it's fish pie for lunch.'

With all of my sisters now married, as Mummy had promised, it was sad that one had already been released from her vows by her husband's untimely death in the waters of the Mediterranean. It left me, 'darling' to everyone, to close up the gap and 'do well'. From now on, attention would be focused on me – spoilt, awkward, nouveau riche, but the last in the line of Leaches. It meant I must do better.

As this awful war came to a messy end it coincided with a change in government, which was quite unable, despite many hopes, to prevent hard times continuing for many people.

I began to fill out, to take account of myself and my shape. As I was, shall we say, top-heavy (not fat, you understand, but endowed with a big front), at school I was allowed to have a bath by myself as I filled the tub to a degree which none of my friends would have been able to share, had they wanted to. I had lost any puppy fat I might have had as I became increasingly aware of my impact on others whether they were boys… or… er… boys.

I was trying to catch up, hopping and skipping just behind the other women in my life, while I attempted to wheedle out answers to those mysterious subjects which only adults talked about. It was a new start for Britain, a world of opportunity lay ahead of me and for the first time in my life, I conceded there might be more to life than rabbits and horses.

4

Emerging From My Chrysalis

This chapter title is not entirely accurate, at least not in the biological sense. When a butterfly emerges from its pupa or chrysalis, it hangs suspended in the warmth, unmoving while its wings expand and dry. For a period of time it does nothing, and it is round about this stage in its life I depart from entomological accuracy. Emerging, nonetheless, from my life as the youngest in the family, a lifetime I was forever in thrall to my 'very sophisticated sisters', I decided I had, at last, something to say with a newfound confidence. I had no intention of waiting while my wings dried, there was too much to see and do. This assurance has always remained with me and emerge, I did.

This confidence was to get me into all sorts of trouble in my life.

Emergence was triggered by the end of World War Two, leaving Sibton empty of its Army clutter and clatter, its carpets tattered and curtains torn, skirtings scuffed and damaged. The rooms echoed eerily as dust motes spiralled up in the morning sun, but my mother had that determined glint in her eye. It spelt out change, and change for the better. Soon my stables would be handed back to me freed of the boxes stamped 'WD' (War Department), the tennis court would have the grass cut, the hard court would be weeded and swept clean, with that happy sound of raised voices bouncing round the bedrooms returning.

With the end of the war Miss Faunce was able to return to Queen's Gate in London. It was decided, foolishly, as it turned out, for me to continue my schooling there, but instead of boarding, I would live with Lizzie in her flat in Addison Court Gardens. The word 'flat' is such a curious name, 'apartment' sounds much grander, but in 1947 it was simply a flat.

I was still woefully lacking in any knowledge of some subjects which today one might think would have been automatically in my curriculum. The hit-and-miss education received to date had caused great gaps in my mind; or sporadic breaches in my general ignorance, I believe, is a more accurate way of describing my education. It wasn't difficult to learn and I enjoyed taking up a subject once I was in front of a teacher who wanted to instil in me a love of knowledge. For me there had never been a day's instruction in geography, for example, and I needed to continue my education in a more professional atmosphere. To be fair to Miss Faunce, the conflict had made it very challenging for her to continue, as teachers kept disappearing off to war. Putting this

altogether and looking to the future in tandem with my reports, Mummy began to realise something must be done.

Being away from my mother's all-seeing eye, and spending evenings with a once-married sister who could explain some of the mysteries of life to me which Mummy would have had considerable difficulty in doing (nor would she have had any intention of doing), meant I grew up more quickly than if I had been living at home. And I tried to match Lizzie's own aspirations. She did not want to remain a widow all of her life, for she was always filled with a sense of joy and fun. It also gave me time to flirt with the Americans still not demobbed from the war.

Alas, news of this reached all the way back home, where my mother was looking into the possibility of finding a new house. She had never liked Sibton with its sad links to a past now abandoned under the frayed rugs. It was evident she wanted a new home without the memories to follow her into the bedroom. While considering her own future, she had been informed of my 'goings-on' with those 'dreadful Americans' and it set alarm bells ringing. This was compounded a few days later when, during my nightly Bible reading (I was fifteen by this time), I put on a well-learnt American drawl. I was summarily dismissed by Mummy, who, furious, said, 'I never want to hear you read the Scriptures again.' To which I arrogantly replied, 'I have been waiting fifteen years to hear that.'

My mother clearly needed to have her teenage daughter supervised twenty-four hours a day and she had just the place for me. Not for the first time in my life, nor by far the last, did

Ximena Leach make an executive decision in which I had no say whatsoever.

*

A judgement was delivered which required me to change any plans I might personally have had, and attend Brondesbury-at-Stocks, an old, established boarding school in the country. As the choice had been made, Mother-to-Headmistress as it were, I had to go along with the change of scenery. There was also the accidental possibility I might pick up some education along the way.

This was a real school out in its own country park in Aldbury, deep in the Hertfordshire countryside. The original establishment, like Miss Faunce's, had been driven out of Surrey, where it had been located since 1865, by the Luftwaffe's random bombing, and Miss Forbes-Dunlop had found a beautiful late Georgian house, once the home of a well-known author, who had filled it with an active salon of intellectual personalities. George Orwell, George Trevelyan the historian and Aldous Huxley were just a few of the literary giants who frequented the place, often staying overnight.

Installed, settling down, I began to look about me and instead of gazing in awe at my peers, I found they not only wanted to make friends but would often seek my advice, especially on those matters picked up from Lizzie. I established myself, started to learn and enjoyed a position of respect, so much so that I began to be noticed by my teachers. It wasn't as if I went out of my way to lead, for some of my friends were quite daunting when it came to pedigree, but I found it stress-

free to get along (no competition to them, I suppose) and make them do as I wanted.

One day my mother received a letter from the headmistress while I was on holiday. The Brondesbury crest was emblazoned on the back of the envelope, which Mother studied curiously as she sought her paper knife.

Dear Mrs Leach

I am very pleased to be writing to you today to let you know that Shirley has been excelling in her work at school. Indeed, she has become so respected by her peers…

At this point Mother looked up at me and smiled: this was more like it. The move to Brondesbury had been the right move and she had been justified in sending her youngest daughter away.

The letter went on:

…so much so we are planning to make Shirley Head Girl as from the autumn term.

The letter ended with many curlicues and felicitations. I suppose, at these fees, one had to fawn occasionally. My mother was totally silent for a moment before exploding as if she were a hidden landmine in the Western Desert. 'Head girl! Shir… er… darling, bring me some notepaper. Quickly! I want to reply *now*.' She was so agitated that she had almost addressed me as 'Shirley' rather than 'Darling'. Mystified, I found a pad of Basildon Bond and read her reply over her shoulder.

Dear Miss Forbes-Dunlop

I am in receipt of your letter proposing that my daughter Shirley be made Head Girl as from the autumn term.

I cannot believe that the standards of Brondesbury have sunk to such a level that she should be propelled to the top of your school and I am removing my daughter as of immediate effect. Please be so good as to have her belongings packed and ready for collection on our arrival.

Yours sincerely

Ximena Leach

I never went back. In a single move, without recourse to my own wishes, I had to leave the school where I was happily engaged with my friends. Protestations were pointless, despite Mother having received a report in which '...*Shirley takes a sophisticated approach to history*.' I wasn't at all sure what it meant but it was a good jingle to drop into my sisters' laps from time to time when we were in discussion about a knotty subject from the past. But a decision had been made and it was final. My case containing my neatly labelled blouses and hockey shorts was collected later, while I was returned to Kent as if I had been a stray cat with the RSPCA.

Like so many things in life, as one door closes another one opens (yet another cliché, I regret), but this particular door was very wide in its opening. I would remind you of my mother's inability to make good gravy, and during the war little had changed with the exception that we had learned a boiled egg needed five minutes' immersion in boiling-hot water. We had

been unable to invite friends back to Sibton for a meal due to the security arrangements in force and even before the war certainly not for a second time, when those invited would all find their diaries magically full. My sisters now saw the opportunity – as clearly as Miltiades the Younger saw the value of the marshes at Marathon – which had been created by my rapid, if not hurried, evacuation from Brondesbury, leaving something of a vacuum in my life. A large crater is another way of describing it, I suppose. Frustratingly, my education was still half-fulfilled, I had no plans for the future and I assumed the only thing for me to do was to marry well and settle down to a life with four children. So, my sisters insisted, verily, demanded, I should go and learn all there was to know about cooking to counteract Mother's extraordinary inability to master a decent gravy for Sunday lunch. Besides, none of them wanted to lose any more friends and as they couldn't cook themselves there had to be someone in the family with the necessary skills. Cinderella, stone floors and the omission of glass slippers described the state of our household at the time.

As a direct result, my first material contact with what would consume my entire life came not from God leaning a muscled arm down from Heaven to send a thunderbolt into my hayloft for a mind, but from the much more prosaic reason of being sent off on a thirty-week course in domestic science at Errollston to learn cookery. And a Catholic cookery course, no less! Errollston was a separate house in the same grounds as the convent, St Mary's, being primarily a convent school in Ascot. I went to learn about domestic science, joining those who were not suited to or interested in an A-level course. Mother had said previously

she had prayed fervently I might become religious but that God had somehow inserted the first letter of the alphabet beforehand and the upshot was I had turned out to be *a*-religious, which was not what she had intended. Perhaps she thought a school with a religious background might prove a stimulus to the lack of religion in my life.

How right she was, bless her, even if it was for all the wrong reasons.

She had been warned that Errollston was a hotbed of Roman Catholics and only a very few girls were Anglicans. This fact made no impression on Mummy, who naturally assumed she could easily deal with 'that sort of thing' if ever it was to arise. I went because she had heard the nuns were very tough on discipline, just the sort of thing Shirley needed, and I would be watched over twenty-four hours of each day! So, boys, Yanks and flirting were placed on hold while I took up another residence.

Errollston had nineteen bedrooms on three floors, with one nun sleeping in another bedroom and one other ensconced in an attic bedroom with sloping walls and skylights. Taking twenty-four of us at a time, girls were sent there by their well-heeled parents in what we now call a 'gap' year, and we cooked all of our own meals, cleaned the place daily and did the laundry, in addition to which we became involved in useful work such as dressmaking. In those days sewing, darning and making one's own dresses were a necessary part of growing up, for most girls made their own dresses and could darn socks and sew on buttons. Many could knit and crochet too. In the evenings we had lectures on the arts and theology following housekeeping, and at the end

of the thirty weeks we would have a five-hour exam which, if we passed, was considered a valuable ticket to many jobs other than secretarial and banking clerical work. The theology lectures were naturally given by the nuns, but as well as their teachings we were able to go to the ballet and drop in on museums once a month in London. It was a happy time.

It is not untrue to say that at home my mother and sisters waited for results, *any* results of my cooking ability, with bated breath, for this was to be a crucial test. Would I make it? Indeed, I found my newfound status as cookery guru – a better phrase is probably 'tentative chefette' – to be called upon at any time of the day, quite pleasant for a change. If ever I stood about for a few minutes a pair of eyes would alight upon me, followed by a wheedling voice uttering half-completed sentences such as: 'You know, darling, that lovely pie you…' And a bit later, as hunger grew: 'Darling, do you remember when you made that…?'

I was becoming increasingly proud of my abilities where food was concerned. The days of being ashamed of the dishes I had attempted were long gone as the rest of the family seized upon me with glee and delight. My boiled carrots with white sauce were talked about as if I had walked to the South Pole alongside Captain Scott. I know boiled carrots in white sauce doesn't sound very exciting these days, what with a thousand cookery books to choose from, written by people with exotic titles such as *The Naked Chef*, for instance, but it was at the time, believe me. My third prize at the village Women's Institute was for a warm (limp) salad and the cause of much celebration. This was as high as gastronomy went in 1947.

So, while we all suffered the worst winter in decades, roads became blocked with reported twenty-foot high snowdrifts and supplies began to dwindle to even less than rationing's tight grip allowed, I considered who I might marry, or at least pondered on the worth of the stock of eligible men, though because of my age I never felt pressured into making a decision. In the meantime, at least we had real gravy.

*

During the time I was still at Errollston I was being prepared for presentation at court. At sixteen I was quite young for this major event in the social calendar but by no means was I the only one in my year, and my mother was determined to see at least one of her daughters presented to His Majesty. It was, after all, in our highly charged lives considered right and proper at the time for those of a certain ilk to do so. I was taught how to curtsy and hold a glass of champagne so the glass did not warm. I was to be presented, packaged up, sold to the world of wealth and privilege and, even more importantly, to the cache of suitors seeking the hand of a rich young lady who was rapidly growing up. *Country Life*, *The Tatler* and *The Illustrated London News* were our almanac, dictionary and calendar, as well as the daily scan of the Court Circular in *The Times*. It was all we needed.

It was one of those days which will remain in my mind for all time simply because it was to be the only time, but, looking back, as one does increasingly the older one gets, the ritual of rich young girls being presented to the monarch was already dying on its feet. The world had been crushed by a simply dreadful

war. England was now poor and a much more egalitarian society. Having emerged triumphant in 1945, Clement Attlee's government found itself with a pyrrhic victory on its hands and one where rationing, which he could do nothing about, would continue for some years to come. People had no time and no money for such displays of excess while all around the bomb craters, half-filled with rubbish, allowed rats to play among the broken bedsteads and rusting car wheels.

I curtsied to Their Majesties and to Princess Margaret along with 400 other girls, as if we were just a factory production line of poupée dolls. Each girl in line was calculating how she could be, in some way, different from the rest so His Majesty would notice her without, of course, stepping out of line in the strict protocol of the day. I was dressed in a strange blue-and-white striped dress purchased from Harvey Nicholls – quite unsuitable, I felt, but chosen by my mother. No surprises there. My hat was navy, also with marigolds on the rim (thankfully, not hollyhocks), making me look like a wasp, but at least I was allowed my first facial. Mother conceded the point as she had one too.

In my opinion, with not much to go on, I have to admit I found King George VI had too much make-up on his face, but his nod at me was gone in a glance as the impatient queue behind me pushed forward and onward like a conga line at the end of an evening's dance. Later, it sprang to mind, to my mortification for getting it so wrong, that our beloved King was much more ill than the public had been informed. Within a few years lung cancer from heavy smoking had taken him, poor man. Princess

Elizabeth was to become Queen long before she was ready for such an enormous task.

And so we bubbled full of champagne and talked too loudly, with accents enough to cut the silk cushions into shreds. The next day I returned to the palace to sign the all-important Register of Debutantes – almost as exciting as the presentation itself. It rounded the 'do' off well.

Astonishingly, the day after this I was transformed back into a real-life Cinderella complete with apron and hot kitchen, for my new life in Moreton-in-the-Marsh in Gloucestershire had begun. I had applied for this job through the *Horse & Hound* magazine as Mother had said she did not want me hanging around in the holidays, so I had obliged her. The role required me to cook for Mrs Smith-Maxwell while attending to thirteen cats, riding horses sent over from Ireland (which I did not enjoy) and anything else which came to mind. One day, a glittering palace in London, rubbing shoulders with the bluest blood in the country; the next, a soiled pinny and limp hair from boiled cauliflower. It was quite a contrast, but probably a good one to remind me, even as Caesar's slave would whisper in his ear, 'You are not a God.'

I never did find my glass slipper.

*

Just a few years later the whole debutante scene had vanished as if it had never been. It was the end of an era, the end of an important date in the social season for the country's elite few. It was right for it to go and it made one more comfortable to

have left those days behind as we settled to a more informal way of living. Besides, women for the first time were beginning to be recognised as more than mere chattels. We could be clever, as well as witty. We could debate skilfully in Parliament, design houses as chartered architects, knock spots off the prosecutors in the courts and generally cause men to reassess their own roles, even as doctors and engineers. Women had flown spitfires in the war, delivering them to the airfields around Britain, and filled shells with high explosives.

There were, though, so many individuals in the country who could see no light in the bleakness of their lives. They had had eight years already and yearned for the good old days before the war so they could forget the awfulness of the Depression and the daily terror of the Blitz. Many women were now without a husband or a lover, but children still had to be brought up and fed, taken to school and loved. There was little time for anything else. Cheerlessness and hopelessness for the future was all so many could expect in those times. The expectancy had been high, once we learned of the surrender. By 1947 it was almost worse than before, with the cold, the dark and the rationing wrapping us in a threadbare shawl.

Mr Cheerful, our new Prime Minister Mr Attlee, summed up the entire nation's position in eighteen words: 'I have no easy words for the nation. I cannot say when we will emerge with easier times.'

Helpful!

People began to grumble for the meat ration had sunk to one shilling a week and potatoes, the cornerstone of most of our lives,

had been placed on the restricted list, meaning mash had to be made from powdered potatoes. So it helped us all in the midst of the grit and grime of our lives when there did come a short respite as Princess Elizabeth married her beau, a Greek Prince, on 20 November 1947.

I was almost able to match this for I had at least met a king and a queen, catered for twelve rabbits and thirteen cats (not a good mix, now I come to think of it) and was finding that I liked cooking and was rather good at it. I was carving out a niche in life.

One doesn't have to be the Oracle of Delphi to realise this could not last for much longer.

I suppose I might have made signs at my sister Pammy's wedding to Stephen Dyboski, a subtle semaphore, that I was comfortable with the Catholic Mass and Catholicism in general. Certainly, I was not speaking out against the Pope as so many people in Britain still did. Soon it would be the turn of the West Indians, but for the time being, 'They're Catholics, they're moving in next door' still gave some a queer tenseness in the stomach almost 500 years after the Reformation, as though some disturbing change might come into their lives. I had my blinkers on, for the nuns at Errollston were ever caring and allowed me to develop my own thoughts as I grew up and showed an interest in their way of life. Nonetheless, at that time I was loyal to my own faith and would cycle to the local C of E church on a Sunday to prove the point.

I should have been more careful, kept quiet at the right times, but of course with my mouth usually wide open, agape like a

guppy, the news that I was enjoying the teachings given by the nuns got back to Mother. It was a repeat of history, a cine film spooling back on itself, for I was removed from my domestic science course before I could learn how to make apple turnovers or even *quenelles de turbotin*. It was one thing to have a son-in-law as a Roman Catholic, another entirely to have one's own daughter seeking to enter the same church. But I was sixteen going on seventeen, determined to have a say in my life and single-minded enough to continue seeking entry into this new way of worship. Leaving Errollston was not quite the end of this story for Mummy in her determined action to protect her daughter. The nuns of Errollston asked for the balance of the year's fee, to be paid as a result of my withdrawal. My mother, bless her, declared, 'Shirley is worth whatever fees I have to pay!' And so she paid up.

I had lasted five months and missed half the course and the exam.

There was to be no peace for a deal had been struck. Mother still wanted me to attend the mother of all finishing schools, greater than those in Paris and Zurich. I was to be a sophisticated young thing so I could land a large catch in the guise of a rich young man in the City. Where else than Cygnets House, an alternative to the customary French finishing establishments? It was founded by Mrs Rennie O'Mahony. She managed to charge $1,325 annual fees, about £32,000 in today's money, though of course that was before all of the extras, which would push that figure into a serious amount of cash.

The school proved to be quite awful. No, on recollection it

was worse: it was *dreadful.* As I have mentioned, Britain was still struggling and for me to be among girls whose only thought was how to balance a pile of books on their heads or worry about their nail varnish confirmed my growing belief this was unacceptable. This world was so far divorced from reality and from the realm I wanted to move towards that I rebelled, and I rebelled after ten days. I flatly refused to go on and my sisters had to come and fetch me.

This was quite a turnabout, the second in four weeks. It placed me in charge of my own destiny for the first time, almost unknown in many ways, a bit scary but very exciting also. As we were saying goodbye to the headmistress, Mrs O'Mahony smiled coldly, eyes having already said goodbye to a lost cause, and said, 'You won't become a swan now, you will always remain a cygnet.'

I replied in the vernacular.

The whole pretence had been triggered by one of the nuns at Errollston. I had asked her one night what she thought of the saying, 'You have to give a life to gain a life'. The sister replied,'If you have learned and understood this, you have learned everything.'

And so the seeds of my vocation had been sown. As Matthew XIII says, 'Some seeds fell on good ground'. It was as though, without realising it, the whole of my short life had been in preparation for this revelation.

In the next two years they would take root.

5

Jeremy Number Three

This was not to say that I did not have fun, nor that I didn't find time to allow boyfriends to enter my life. Up until now I had been an expert flirt and was accomplished at being *very sweet*. Not a great deal of use when you think about it and what does 'sweet' mean anyway? For the future, I made up my mind I was going to do less flirting, employ more subtlety and supply less sweetness. When you are just seventeen and post-war by a couple of years there is not exactly a wealth of experience to be able to fall back on, but two of my sisters were now married, the third had experienced the joy of marriage and I could see the bliss in having one's own home, cooking for a family, setting one's own direction in life rather than following the programme drummed into me by a succession of controlling women, even though I loved them all very much.

When you have three older sisters, sophisticated to a high degree, who urge you, daily, to find a nice young man, there is no doubt the peer pressure is considerable and unrelenting. I was sitting at the very edge of my nest, the abyss below me holding me back, yet I pecked at any approaches made by anyone who came near as I fluttered my new wings, which were drying fast in the wind like that proverbial butterfly.

Having been presented at court it was assumed I was on a billboard, *the* market. The word was out; a name appeared on a list for appropriate suitors to mull over while demolishing Martinis, having gone up to university to read Greats or Humanities. Because of this migration of potential husbands to Oxford and Cambridge it was felt that I should follow them, but there was a problem. I am sure you are aware by now, and have made up your minds, that my education was sketchy at best, pretty awful at worst. A tutor was needed to coax me out of my daydreaming and prepare me for the exams. One duly arrived on command. Rather like a clockwork toy he lasted for a while, earnestly driving me through the vagaries of syntax and the location of Timbuctoo, but like all mechanical things he finally began to wind down as I moved into position and made eyes at him mercilessly.

It was ground-hog day all over again. My mother, on learning of the apparent stalemate in my tuition, called me in. 'You are absolutely disgraceful,' she concluded and so ended any plans that had been made for me to attain a double first at Cambridge.

*

JEREMY NUMBER THREE

I had had a doll for what seemed like forever: his name was Jeremy. Now I had another – Jeremy, that is, not another doll. His father was a banker, Glyn Mills and Co. We both had a passion for hunting and dancing. As time went on there was an assumption on my part we might get married one day, and have a jolly good wedding. It wasn't yet a plan, just something I felt that this was the start of the rest of my life.

I did, however, enjoy male company and Jim – yes, Jim – was also in our gang. Jim was good at jitterbugging, an essential attribute for a man. Well, anyone who wanted to go out with me for an evening. He loved horses as I did, and invited me to stay at his parents' estate in Ireland for a weekend. Dressing for dinner that first evening I inadvertently pressed the maid's bell instead of the light switch, following which, after a pause, a flustered member of staff arrived. I was asked what she could do for me and, being warned that we would be wearing long for dinner, I asked her to help me now she had taken the trouble to climb up the giant staircase at my bidding.

Downstairs at dinner, somewhat delayed, my hostess, Jim's mother, asked me rather pointedly, 'Do you have a lady's maid at home?' I said, 'Oh heavens no, not for years, since before the war!' The lady of the house looked annoyed. 'Well, it was *my* cook who came up to you, slowing the entire meal down, so that's why there is a delay.' At this I studied the tablecloth, admiring the fine weave of the cloth. I was duly chastened and soon after, Jim disappeared, his departure hastened by my cooling ardour.

As we were now hunting in packs, it wasn't long before another appeared on the horizon, Jeremy Number Three. Another

inauspicious beginning, it also happened to overlap with the departure of Number Two.

*

Jeremy Chittenden's family had had a fine house in Sandwich, Kent. When the German bombers were unable to find London one night, they released their bomb loads and reduced the house to rubble. It caused an immediate enforced move, so the family decamped to a rented house in Ireland to last out the war, safe from further anguish. Jeremy, however, on the equivalent of a gap year before going up to Cambridge to read Agriculture at Trinity, felt it would be invaluable to work on a farm, which just so happened to be not far from where we lived. This allowed his mother to write to mine (who both knew the other from a previous spell), asking if he could come over from time to time on his day off. The bonus would be in the fact he could play the piano 'divinely'.

My immediate impression of Number Three was that he was rather ugly and quite boring at times as he was forever suggesting we do the crossword. Boring is not a modern teenager idiom but one I was very familiar with in 1949. Although he had a rumpled face, he would be painted in oils later in life by his daughter, and his portrait was to hang in the Mall Galleries in London for an exhibition. There was something in his face which merited a few shillings' worth of oil paint and canvas. Besides, it was painted by his future daughter.

A good portrait perhaps, but unlike the other two men in my life, Jeremy was a hopeless dancer with two uncoordinated left feet.

We would arrive at a debutantes' ball, stay for a short while before moving speedily through the other dancers to the edge of the floor, departing to drive around the countryside in his Lagonda, which had an annoying habit of squirting oil in all directions.

At one dance, a memorable occasion, I was asked to dance by a Robin Lee-Pemberton, who went on to become Governor of the Bank of England.

'So, what do you do, Robin?' I asked over his shoulder, glad to be dancing with one right and one left foot.

'I am doing Greats at Trinity,' came the reply.

'Oh,' I said, somewhat flattened but needing to fill a long pause, which I felt I had created. 'Oh, are you cleaning grates in the university?'

Robin controlled a guffaw, seeing I was serious. 'Not grates, *Greats*. You know, *Literae Humaniores—*'

'What? Er, excuse me?'

'The Classics, Philosophy, Ancient History.'

Hole, deepest and blackest, came to mind in quick succession. But Robin was smiling.

'I do hope you don't mind if I dine out on that one for a while. I'm not being rude, I just think it is very funny, you imagining me cleaning grates for the undergrads rooms, to earn money, I suppose. I must remember to say "reading Greats" rather than "doing Greats".'

We remained good friends and indeed, not only did he dine out on this for many years to come but I also managed to spin it up a bit myself as well.

Little by little, annoyingly at first, Jeremy Number Three

grew on me like lichen takes time to cover a granite gatepost, until I looked round and weekends had become important days. When it meant coming back to the house for a night, he always managed to leave something behind accidentally after he left, but he was fooling no one when he called the next week to claim, with a nonchalant air, his pair of gloves or his bowler hat, items he would have found difficult to forget, being so used to having them with him at all times. In fact, Jeremy without his bowler would have made him look unnatural had I met him out shopping bare-headed.

There were others in the gang at the beginning. I was invited to attend a Mass at Folkestone church one Sunday morning. I thought idly it could prove interesting and went along to see what a Catholic Mass was all about. It was very different to my C of E service, a lot of what I might have described as mumbo-jumbo as I did not read Latin, and this contrasted with the beautiful thousand-year-old church which I attended each Sunday. It was odd, bearing in mind my future life, that the visit had no impact on me at all or at least, nothing I wanted to retain, and almost no memory of it remains in my mind today.

The man who took me was a friend, one of our group who were seen out together and enjoyed each other's company. Jeremy was something else. As Mr Chittenden and Miss Leach began to be an item I felt it only fair and proper to write to my alter ego, Jeremy Two, putting him in the picture, despite the loss of his companionship while hunting and dancing this would entail. It felt right to do so and a letter duly went off to him. I received a letter back, saying, '*I didn't know you cared so much*', which I

didn't, but he had somehow misinterpreted my words. However, I was now free, unattached and beginning to fall for this other man just as another issue loomed over the horizon. My mother was making none-too-subtle hints she was not at all happy with our growing relationship.

'Darling,' she would say with a pause, 'darling... *they* have cocktail parties...' and 'I have learned *they* have a house in the south of France of all places...' and even 'Jeremy's father is President of the Sandwich Golf Club... for goodness' sake!' Her eyes would travel heavenward. Yet we were the *nouveaux riches*.

Mother, of course, was jealous for by this time I had become very fond of Jeremy's parents, who had a close relationship with their son. At the beginning of our courtship I thought I was closer to Jeremy than his own parents until one day I asked if I could meet them. I was calmly, if carefully, rebuffed.

'Oh, not yet, I think. I don't want you to meet them for a little while as they are such wonderful people and I don't know you well enough.'

I was quite hurt – well, *very* hurt on the inside – but determined he would soon know me well enough. Within a short while his father would replace the space once occupied by my real father, for my memory of Daddy was sketchy at the very least.

All this constant talk of Jeremy and what we did together preyed on my mother's mind. Was Darling being careful? Was she drinking too much? Was she keeping up the standards expected of a Leach? What did we do in that car of his when we went out all evening rather than stay behind to do the crossword? And why was there oil on my evening gown?

Mummy had developed a characteristic of talking out loud to herself when she wanted to resolve something in her mind. It would emerge in the most bizarre places. One day she was taking a bath when Jeremy and I were sitting cross-legged outside the bathroom in a linen store, but don't ask me why we were there, for I have no idea.

'She's seeing too much of him,' came clearly across the steam and the door panel. 'It's not good at all.'

Jeremy chuckled to himself quietly while I became even more determined to control my own life.

Neither could she stop the fun. Without a vocation but moneyed, Jeremy would lark about, finding mischief out of life itself. At the Dublin Horse Show he bought a red hat from Dunhill's and proceeded to walk about, introducing himself as the Peruvian Ambassador, complete with swagger bow and a false Spanish accent. To keep up with him I would pat my clothes in place, examine my own hat in a mirror and generally take ages as I went through the familiar ritual of determining what to wear. Poor Jeremy must have waited for hours and hours during the time I knew him, as I hummed and hawed, facing my opened wardrobe, placing endless scarves or blouses in front of me in despair. In the end, having told me it was all a bit of a waste of time, he announced, after a particularly long wait, 'I'll cure you of this', which I forgot all about until he turned up at the next dance in a boiler suit and not surprisingly was turned away at the door. So much for the experiment.

His sense of fun did not extend to his mother's fine sense of the rightness of things and the place in society for everyone.

With Christmas coming up, she gave all of her staff a present: a new uniform. I can imagine none of them would have been too enamoured with such a gift even if they had been quality outfits. Perhaps they received something else on the day itself?

The focus, though, was on the two of us as we continued to tighten the links which bound us together and on his return from a visit to Switzerland, two years after we had met, Jeremy began to call me 'Bunny' and we tumbled almost in slow motion into a deep, warm relationship. While it is so easy for one to say, 'We are very close' without examining those words carefully, Peter Ryecroft, a good friend and one of the pack, who went on to become an exalted eye surgeon, clarified my own words. He said, 'If anything were to happen to you two, I would stop believing in love.' Yes, we were now very close, as close perhaps as a tuppeny stamp is to an envelope.

To keep a few secrets to ourselves, we would send coded telegrams to each other, splitting words into pieces so no one, other than *les amoureux*, and, perhaps Bletchley Park, would understand. I would find the poor telegram boy cycling all the way up to the house only to keep him waiting while I decoded a message delivered into my hot little hand and wrote a new one to be returned forthwith. Complete nonsense, of course, but in those first heady days of freedom, the privacy of a telegram meant a great deal to us both.

Filling my spare time, occupying my mind, beginning to understand this very dear man, I discovered Jeremy had a strong underlining belief in God, and God with him. At times it was as though his faith was more resilient than my own. We, of course,

remained within the Church of England, but I was continuing to be motivated by new ideas, ideas I wanted to learn more about, of a faith far older than the one I belonged to. I continued to attend the same church each week because we had always done so as a family. It is natural to do so and even when I made the change, I felt in many ways I was comfortable in talking of either faith. I was, as it were, becoming bi-lingual.

Eventually, and quite early in Jeremy's mind, I had passed whatever obstacles I needed to jump so I could be invited to Wingfield, his parents' home in Ireland. The first time is always an acid test to anyone in the same situation and it does not get easier as new generations arise and take over this moment when one is placed under the lens of a microscope. Everyone knows why you are there but nothing is said at the time. This is, after all, the first gathering, a convention almost, though not in the business sense, which could lead to possible, potential, prospective parents-in-law and, on the other side, prospective daughter-in-law. To be fair, neither of us had thought along this route yet, or perhaps Jeremy had but had not told me. It was nice, though, to meet the couple he felt so strongly about. This was especially true in my case as Jeremy did not as a rule bring girlfriends home to impress his parents. The first night I was dry-mouthed at dinner but determined to shine. The table was beautifully laid with placemats at each chair, showing pictures of humming birds, very similar to ours at home.

'Oh!' I exclaimed, with the remembrance of Sibton's table. As our whole family had always been actresses of one sort or another, which gave us iron nerves, it allowed me with my eyes

shining to say, 'Oh, humming birds!' with some force as I looked across at the family studying me carefully.

A slight pause, quick glances from father to mother. Jeremy studied his side plate as if it contained a dead wasp.

'Salmon flies,' said his father, my possible, potential father-in-law. '*Salmon flies.*'

Oh, the agony of youth. How could I get it so wrong? I blushed so that the tips of my ears burnt like a brush fire – I did so want this first meeting to be a success.

There are times when you are young, you just wish the earth would open up like an earthquake and swallow you whole so you can disappear from sight. I had to assume that a salmon fly was associated with fishing of which I knew little, so it was better to keep my peace, look suitably humbled and try to steer the conversation on to subjects I knew something about. Rabbits, perhaps, or riding? Would it be going too far if I told them I was involved in capturing a Messerschmitt pilot? But the visit ended well and I began to see why Jeremy was so fond of his parents. Despite the story of the staff Christmas presents they were warm, exceptional people, who placed me quickly at my ease. I can only assume they liked me as much as I began to love them. Their adopted names applied by their children were 'Ma-fir' and 'Pa-fir', nicknames which I adopted.

When I returned home it was to find my mother in the throes of lists and notes, having found a new house: Ringleton Manor, near Sandwich, Kent. Ringleton was two houses grown together in soft, aged brick, approached by a long drive. There were seven bedrooms, too large really for my thinking, for the family had

spread its wings a long time before, but Mother insisted on two drawing rooms *and* a library and some stabling for Whisky my horse, although as I was away for most of the time there was little opportunity for riding.

It necessitated a move in the hard winter of 1947. Due to the condition of the house following the war it had to be refurbished before we could move in. This required us to decamp, tearfully for me, from Sibton, and the two of us went to stay at the Bull Inn at Eastry, a sixteenth-century pub with a white rendered facade alongside the main road. They put up with Mother's foibles, the loud voices and the demands, because we were good business at a time of struggle all over the country.

Mummy was able to supervise the refurbishment works, probably ignoring the architect's pleas for her to let him know when revisions had been made directly to the builder. But finally it was all done to her satisfaction and we moved in, along with the horse and a mountain of what, suspiciously, gave the impression of junk, though much of this was moved to an enormous barn, which now acted as a storeroom. It was a clean sweep, no memories of the past; the smell of new paint coupled with that hollow reverberation in each room before the curtains and pictures are hung. There was a lonesomeness about the new house, beautiful as it was with its gardens and lake, and now not even a trace of Father existed. He had gone from us all, and I was thankful I had Jeremy as my anchor in life.

While we drove round the countryside at the weekends attending hunt balls and dinner parties, there grew in me my need to change my faith, to give up the Church of England,

which I had known since I was able to walk. It had become an option I could not put off any longer for it was in my sleep and in my thoughts throughout the waking day. Changing my faith was perhaps not the right phrase, certainly not the idea I want to put over, for my Mother's faith, Anglicanism, had many of the philosophies I could continue to support, but I needed something more and my Church simply did not have that strong suit I sought. We were Low Church, that curious term separated by ritual and ceremony from High Church. I wanted to find a special path in life and Catholicism provided me with a clear route forward, something I knew would satisfy me deep down inside.

As always, jungle drums had been beating. Kent was such a small place, having always been able to send out early signals since the approach of the French fleet of Francis the First, almost 500 years earlier. Notice of my impending move reached the ears of our local vicar – who else? – and I was approached after Matins one Sunday.

'Ah, Shirley! Nice to see you here as usual. Perhaps you would like to come to Confession?'

His inference was peculiar, bearing in mind Confession was a commonplace in the Catholic faith but not in the Church of England. There was a clear indication I was going to be tackled on my Catholic interest. Had I been one of my sisters, I might have replied, 'Not bloody likely!' My head nodded in a most demure fashion as if taking a great deal of weighty consideration to accept his very nice offer, rather as Tory members nod their heads in agreement with everything their PM has to say at the

Dispatch box. Eventually, I threw him a winning smile: 'No, thank you, Vicar.'

Somewhat chastened that an eighteen-year-old girl had rebuffed what was essentially a command in those days, he being one of the pillars of society along with the bank manager and the doctor, he could only offer a tight-lipped response, 'I will be ready to receive you back in the Church in due course.'

It was never to be.

But it almost didn't happen, that is me changing to becoming a Catholic. At the time I was, I must admit, having a fun stretch, so I wrote to the nuns saying I was not going to bother for the moment as I was having a ball. Well, it was the truth though I didn't say it quite in those words. They replied in their own fashion: 'Grace is given for a certain time and if you do not respond now, it might never be given.' I leapt on a horse as if delivering the mail to Kansas City for Wells Fargo and dashed to the nearest Catholic Church. There I found a priest and gave him my problem.

'I *am* to become a Catholic.'

'I very much doubt it,' he replied.

Not a good start, I felt, to the conversion.

To which I had a ready answer now: 'It's all to do with Grace, Father.'

He gave me a book and told me to come back in three months' time. What he had given me was a penny catechism, which I thought was as good as it gets in those days.

Eventually I was received into the Roman Catholic Church with my mother and cleaner as witnesses. Mummy was very good

holding her peace as I made the proclamation, so I bumbled the words 'abjuring all other faiths', for she was still a devout Anglican. At the back of the church for Confession with the priest, who did not want my mother to attend, I was asked to say yes or no to the Ten Commandments. And that was the end of it. The next day I took a train to Ascot and made my first Holy Communion.

I was in.

*

Once Ringleton had been refurbished in *Country Life* stylish mode, the new vicar of the village was eventually invited for Easter Sunday lunch. Still in wartime rationing, we had saved up a Christmas pudding, now renamed 'plum-duff', probably best served with brandy butter, though where we could have got the butter from heaven knows. It was all consumed with evident pleasure; this despite Mother having quite forgotten this pudding, which had hung about forgotten on a shelf since… well… well past its sell-by date. On being challenged on its age earlier in the week, she retorted, while blowing dust off the torn brown paper wrapping with loud exhalations, that the brandy inside would prevent it absorbing any bugs. Evensong came a few hours later, at which time, in succession, Mummy and then Didi had to disappear carefully, if somewhat speedily, through the south door, only to be followed by the Vicar himself, making his excuses through desperate eyes.

The service was delayed.

For the first time since the end of the war the future laid a

soft mantle on my earlier, frantic mind. I could see that once Jeremy had passed through Trinity at Cambridge I would become a farmer's wife. He had been working long hours on the gap-year farm and, with our move to Ringleton, it was still near enough for us to remain in local contact, especially with Jeremy's car to hand.

Up until now all thoughts had been developing on marriage, centring on a white wedding, but I was badly shaken, more than I could fathom why, when Isabel, a very good friend of mine, got married. She turned to me, on the day, gloriously happy.

'It's your turn next year, Shirley.'

What I should have done was to give her a kiss and agree with her with a silly grin on my face for that was, after all, what was going to happen. It was in the stars – awful phrase, I know, but it will have to do. Instead, for some unknown and unnerving feeling there was a blankness, a barren mood, something unidentified floating in the back of my mind as it attempted to tell me something vital, like the decoding of one of our telegrams. Each time, trying to focus, the feeling collapsed into an annoying pink haze, which I put down to too much champagne. So all I could do was smile at Isabel and throw confetti at her to cover my confusion. I was only nineteen at the time – perhaps it was growing pains?

That night, brooding alone in my bed over the fact that as I was converting to Catholicism, perhaps this could make me appear different to some of my friends who had not made the leap in faith as I had? Or was it an impending sixth sense of having my life cut short by some catastrophe or other? It was certainly difficult, in the dark hours of the night, to see my

golden horizon, which had risen each dawn without fail in the last few months. In the end I gave notice to my exhausted mind to take a break and finally sleep came, where there were dreams of black jealousy as I studied Jeremy huddled over the ubiquitous crossword with his mother.

These pressures mounted. The result became almost inevitable and then certain. External forces, stresses, call them what you wish, piled into a sky of tension. My mother, bless her, recognised the signs, understanding the strength of my new faith, and whisked me off to Rome. This was the year of the Festival of Britain, with the King now very ill. Opening the festival was to be his last public appearance with the Queen. While he launched the Skylon and the Dome of Discovery we sweltered in the Italian summer and attended Mass, me having been poured into a new black dress despite the heat. Mother and I both wore mantillas to show we were fully committed to the service. I felt over-dressed for, across the seats from us, worshippers wore short-sleeved blouses and shorts much to Mummy's dismay at the show of disrespect, which was instantly heightened when a farmer brought in a pig on a lead on his way to market.

Mother whispered, *sotto voce* – more *voce* than *sotto*, I fear – 'They simply have no self-control, do they?' This remarkable incident was bettered the next day when we managed to attend Mass in St Peter's, the Holy of Holies and a truly wondrous church. We had been told firmly before the service on no account were we to speak or call out as the Pope passed us in the main aisle as he processed, but the vast congregation erupted as soon as he appeared, quite ignoring earlier pleas.

'*Viva Papa! Viva Papa!*' they chanted in unison, genuflecting towards him in sheer joy at his presence.

At this Mother started up again with evident dismay. 'You have been told not to speak out!' she exclaimed in loud English – the equivalent of soft Italian, I presume – as she sought to fulfil the request for everyone to remain calm. 'No self-control, that's the problem.' She might have added, for all I know, 'No wonder we won the war', but I had switched off in embarrassment by then, disowning her completely.

I arrived back in Britain calmer and more settled to learn that the King had had a part of his lung removed. It did not look good for the Royal Family, and after all he had done in the war to keep our spirits up. Mummy understood cancer and she could see only a very short life left for him.

Nor did it look too rosy for our government, for although Winston Churchill was back in power he had been forced to send 6,000 troops to Egypt in late 1956 to deal with the anti-British disturbances at the Suez Canal.

Jeremy welcomed me back with a hug and I returned to Ringleton with the future very clear. I was focused, as the young like to say today. Focused perhaps, but exasperated also when I found Mummy leaning out of a first-floor window, looking down on the huge barn of ours, shouting at some men who were removing various objects of furniture from the building.

Unclear of what instructions she had given the builders, she enquired in her *nice* voice, 'Have you got everything you want? *Do* come in and have something to eat when you have finished.'

Didi hissed from behind the curtain: 'No, Mummy. They're actually stealing from us. They're burglars!'

Mother said, 'Are they, darling? How extraordinary!'

It was this sort of character which endeared her to us, despite her presiding over the family as if she were the Admiral of the Fleet.

I had to wait. Like Pammy it was considered *right* to create a gap between engagement and marriage so I could come to terms with the whole commitment and for 'the sake of appearances, darling'. There was, in those days, the ongoing dread of babies born out of wedlock and a clear signal had to be sent to all friends that I was pure and chaste and had waited. We had been engaged unofficially for some time but no announcement had been made in the Press for I was only now twenty years old. This may seem very young today, with careerists leaving marriage and babies to the very last minute, but in 1951 girls began to feel they were on the shelf if they were not married by the age of twenty-two or three. It didn't matter to me, for the time was filled with plans and I had already learned the marriage vows off by heart.

There came a day when I had to recount to Jeremy with an embarrassed giggle as I brought him up to date on a visit I had had from Geoffrey, my brother-in-law. Geoff had suggested he introduce Jeremy to a very nice prostitute – to gain some experience in those matters we had never gleaned from our parents in the past. Sex education at school was the dissection of a frog and the examination of the private parts of the Clouded Yellow under a magnifying glass. Naturally, Geoffrey's kind offer

was turned down as I was not sure this was the kind of thing engaged couples would need to discuss.

'That won't be necessary, Geoffrey, thank you,' I replied with a flushed face while wondering how my turn-off would be interpreted, or rather, misinterpreted. Whatever he thought, I knew nothing had occurred between Jeremy and I on that score.

How different it all was to the casualness of today's relationships.

*

During this time of whirlwind excitement, which now included being a fully paid-up member of the Roman Catholic Church, I had been invited back to Errollston, this time as an assistant teacher in Domestic Science following a short spell at St Mary's in Hampstead. I simply adored teaching and never lost my love of educating children, widening their horizons and bringing to them a purpose in their young lives. As part of my job I had to monitor lunchtimes and private study called 'corrections'. When taking the class for this homework period, with all the girls' heads bent towards their desks in earnest study – don't forget these children were some of the brightest in the country – I would sometimes hum a piece of music, possibly a number from The Beatles, regrettably often out loud. There would be speedy protests from the class within a very short time.

'Do your corrections please, Sister, we want good marks.'

From time to time I was also asked to teach on Justice and Peace, two noble subjects on which we could all dwell, but I would tell my girls there was precious little justice and absolutely no peace at all, which would make us all smile before getting

down to the real work again. It was this warm, loving relationship we had for each other which made the days fly past.

Having earlier told my mother that I wanted to work with prostitutes… though that might not have been a very good way of putting this – it perhaps needed further explanation. I should have explained immediately there was a need in my mind to be able to see if I could help them break free of the bonds holding them to their profession. Thinking about it, I have no idea how this ideal could be achieved. Suffice to say Mummy decided that I needed to go somewhere where I could teach my cooking skills rather than tramp dismal streets, making suggestions to the girls.

So I went back to Errollston and moved into room number six, a nice bedsitter set aside for teaching staff. I was away from Ringleton and doing what I loved while planning my whole future, word perfect in my marriage vows and sorting out my bottom drawer.

As we turned into 1952, the King gave up his struggle against lung cancer. A queen came to the throne at the moment of his death and I would become twenty-one that year. As I looked ahead to my new life, freed from the ties of my family though having future bonds to a loving husband and vows to keep, I could see nothing but happiness on the horizon.

6

The Sun On My Desk

I had called in to an auction house in North Ascot and seen some nice imitation Chippendale dining chairs, just the sort of thing for our new life together. Jeremy would need to be told so he could make the decision for me to make a bid. Having decided to write, there was just enough time to get the letter off before I was called for tea downstairs. At six I was due to teach my students – Supper Cooking.

My desk built into a cupboard was close to the window so the light shone across the top. It was 4 p.m. and I remember it was a nice day in the February of 1952, the 4th, with the low winter sun still dazzling on the horizon such that it was reflecting off the paper into my eyes. My heart was full of goodness towards my fellow beings.

It was a moment in time, an instant only, when the flow of

words petered out as I deliberated on what to say to finish up after proposing I put in a bid for the chairs. My hand began to write again but of its own volition. This time my mind was controlling my pen but my thoughts were being controlled by something else. I wrote:

'*But there seems no point now as I am to be a nun.*'

I sat staring at the words, still wet with ink as the heavens opened. The line of verse was earth-shattering, overwhelming. I wanted to drown, appalled as I was at the nakedness of the truth facing me. It was the word '*am*' which mattered; it was the only word which mattered. I hadn't attempted to put down something softer, such as 'I would like to' or even 'I want to be', but 'I *am* to be a nun', which allowed no room for compromise. The feeling inside me was so strong that I knew with absolute certainty I would never now be married, I would never have children, never wed Jeremy and have him hold me in his arms. At this I sobbed. How could God take away my life? At the happiest time in my life I had been asked to give it all up. I do remember later saying to myself that I wished I had said yes with courtesy, but at this point my mind had blanked out everything else with the immediacy of the moment.

God had chosen me, a fool, a lightweight, to serve Him. It was incomprehensible yet I also recognised this was something which had been planned for all eternity. Everything began to make sense; all those uncertainties of the past when I had become aware of something or someone just in the wings, guiding my everyday actions. It had all come to a conclusion.

Then all the other issues came tumbling down as if a sudden gust of wind had blown my carefully built house of cards into the gutter. My mother, my sisters, the wedding arrangements, Jeremy's wonderful parents who I adored, and above all, Jeremy himself. My eyes swelled up so I was hardly able to see. I had missed tea, I realised, when there came a knock at my door. One of the nuns had come to find me.

'Whatever is the matter?' She stared into my ravaged face, the uncontrollable shaking in my shoulders, my hands trembling as if I had Parkinson's. Between the tears I managed to say, 'There's not going to be a wedding.'

The nun frowned. 'I'm so sorry, my dear, but—'

I cut her off rather too fiercely, I fear: 'But you have no part in this. This is between Jeremy, God and me.'

The nun retreated quickly, hoping I would come downstairs for teaching at six. At the time I have to admit it was doubtful.

This call, this revelation, this terrible shock, which others would describe with a hundred different labels of their own making in the future – some understanding what had happened, others scornful, believing I had cold feet over the wedding – this was not as it should have happened. There had been no whirl of a wind, no puffy cloud on which angels sat, no shaft of bright light let alone a heavenly choir, just the simple but irreversible words on the notepaper written in my own hand.

Eventually, after what seemed like a million years, I pulled myself into some sort of shape, sealed the letter and walked down the stairs, where I left it to be posted. Removing it from my hand was another irrevocable action for it established my fate and

all I could do was imagine the state of Jeremy when he opened the envelope up with his usual smile of anticipation at his girl's latest missive.

What did she want now?

It was, I have to admit, a struggle when I arrived in the kitchen, saying good evening to the eight students, averting my eyes and finding it hard to concentrate on my work. Two nuns looked in on me, having learned, I'm sure, of my calamity, but seeing me there in front of the class, they withdrew silently, just as dark shadows leave a church as a door opens, leaving me to my inner thoughts and a life now lost forever.

That night I lay on my back, studying the patterns of light on the ceiling. Every so often my hands and legs trembled uncontrollably. There was fear for Jeremy and fear for my future life. It was as though I had fallen between two high cliffs as I hung suspended in a blackness so intense I couldn't see my fingers in front of my nose. It was a coalmine without a Davy lamp. Jeremy floated above me with a sad face as he stared at a letter covered with my tears. But it made no matter; it was done.

The following day I went to Mass and heard the words: 'See your vocation'. It ended with: 'So you have nothing to boast about, I will be your virtue, your Holiness and above all, your freedom.'

The die was cast.

*

'Drop everything, I'm coming round!' It was Jeremy's anxious voice on the phone. 'I've had your letter.'

So he knew. He arrived in his car in a flurry of stone chippings and we drove out to Windsor Park and walked and talked for hours on end. I told him again what had happened, about the phrase '*I am to become a nun*' not '*I want to become a nun*', and my fears for the future. He replied, 'That letter was not written by the Bunny I know.'

'Oh Jeremy, take me away from all this! Take me away to the ends of the world.'

The words were dreadfully trite, pointless, merely there to help anchor me to this dear man for a few more hours. He was quiet, never angry, and in the end he stopped me on the path and turned to face me.

'If this is between me and God, I know who is going to win.'

It was as if he had a perfect understanding of God, better than myself. His silent, discreet strength stole across to me and entered my soul. He made me wonder if I should have been more positive at the time of receiving my mission. Who knows now? I reacted in the way I did because without a shadow of a doubt my actions would bring about enormous change, so full of trauma in fact I had no idea if I could handle it. It was literally a bolt out of the blue. I was just twenty. Now I would have to cancel my arrangements to marry, speak to what would have been my parents-in-law and explain to them; justify my actions to my sisters and my mother, who would not believe I was serious.

After Jeremy had spoken to me I felt easier, more settled in my mind, which up until then had been a mess of jumbled sheets on too small a bed; he knew, and he accepted it. Yes, I was going to lose a life, but I was going to gain one as well. It was to be my

founding principle from that day on. I clung to it, its absolute rightness a safe raft on a very rough sea.

News leaked out slowly that any plans we had for a wedding were well and truly cancelled, although it was not my intention. I wanted to gauge the right time. A priest I knew well was furious: 'You have no right to cancel your wedding plans. And, if you did, what sort of a nun do you think you would make? I suppose you are going to be a Carmelite?'

'No,' I answered truthfully. 'I want to enter the Institute of the Blessed Virgin Mary, the IBVM.'

A Jesuit priest also in attendance in the room interrupted, 'That's quite sensible.' His words were a sedative to me in an otherwise hostile world of misunderstanding. For this sort of thing didn't happen in post-war Britain. It was to many incomprehensible, just an over-excited young girl still in a world of ponies and wealth, and I was reminded on several occasions by friends in the same group of Peter Ryecroft's comments on eternal love. Deep down it hurt very much for there was nothing I could do to change the situation.

The stresses and strains eventually told on us all. It was quite awful. Jeremy's parents repeatedly begged me to change my mind, simply unable to comprehend what I had done and for what reason. How could I compare marrying their son with being a nun? It made no sense to them at all. They might go to church each week and praise the Lord at the right times, but to cancel one's marriage plans for life apart in a nunnery?

'This is inexplicable,' they argued. The pain of the discussions could not be overstated, for Jeremy's father had replaced my real

father, who was no more than a memory. He was 'Pa-fir' to me, a father I could trust. Certainly a relationship of daughter-in-law to father-in-law had built up that went beyond that which might be thought reasonable. It hurt him as much as did my own unhappiness. I did not take it in at the time, or perhaps I did but there were so many other problems to address that the chaos that ensued in my family was missed or watered down in my mind.

My sisters had simply not believed I was prepared to give up the life I knew for an unknown and frankly, to them, alarming world, misunderstood by most and not helped by various Hollywood films, such as Kathryn Hulme's book converted to celluloid, *The Nun's Story*, which was a lot harsher and more judgemental than anything seen in the film with Audrey Hepburn, or Monica Baldwin's book, *I Leap Over the Wall*. Those were screening in the cinemas even as my problems were falling into their laps. It was one thing for them to tell me I would be back in six weeks, another to realise I was serious and nothing was going to change my mind. My confirmation of my wishes to them implied the loss of their youngest sister, for always.

With all of this upset it was perhaps not surprising Jeremy only received a Third at Trinity, a pretty awful result. He had heard on the day of the May Ball; a day which should have been so good for him was a disaster and he was devastated by the news. I was cruelly to blame, and my future in-laws, people that I adored, now turned, saying, 'Thank you, darling, for upsetting a young man's life.'

The dam burst and Jeremy was sent off to Rhodesia, ironically to what seemed like the ends of the world where I myself had wanted to go.

I went to see Lizzie in London and poured out my heart, explaining I was not only going to lose Jeremy and I was not to be married, but I would lose my family, my mother and my sisters. Mother had not yet been told and it was time I took the plunge.

'I can only see you three times a year,' I said through tear-filled eyes.

'You have to go and see Mummy, darling. She'll understand, I know.'

Arriving at the house, my chin firm, I said to my mother: 'Mummy, I have something to say to you.' I thought she had probably considered the whole cancellation of the wedding was due to something hidden as yet from view. I was right.

'Yes, darling. You are going to have a baby, I expect.'

'No, no, Mummy. I'm going to be a nun.'

Mother looked up, eyebrows rising like the sun over the Sahara. She was not expecting this change of events. 'I'd rather you were going to have a baby. I can deal with that,' she told me. But she remained calm and in control, not attempting in any way to try and change my mind. I loved her for it.

The change I had undergone lay deep: the metamorphosis had not yet shown on the surface though below the skin modifications were already under way. It came to pass that there was only one person in the country who truly understood me, the one who had let me go. Although it would be a long-lasting, painful time, Jeremy was clear in his own mind. It was right for me to continue along the chosen path despite, as it appeared, most of the world clamouring to be the first to say, 'It will never work, Shirley.'

Jeremy, alone, remained steadfast.

I had a visit from, of all people, my bank manager, who came round to see me, enquiring if I was all right. I was touched that such a man, busy and serious as he was, could take the time out to tend to one of his customers. It is not something, I believe, we would be likely to see these days.

The final knife thrust came just at a time I needed support from my fellow Catholics. It was to hear a Jesuit priest echoing the Errollston nun, telling me in straight talk that I had no right to say I would not be marrying Jeremy, 'as if you have any part in the decision.'

The priest could not understand the strength of my calling and was thinking only that I had made a promise to Jeremy that I was now breaking. In the sixties this was not considered acceptable behaviour. But there had been no official engagement.

Mother took me off to Spain for I had even remonstrated with a nun who had only tried to help me by saying how sorry she was.

'God is always near you,' the nun added in a helpful tone.

'God's not complicated,' I said with suppressed rage. 'God is not near me, He is *with* me.'

Mother had waited until the end of the ten-week term to allow me to complete my teaching contract. I was then whisked off to Madrid with plans to head south to the beaches of the Mediterranean.

Out of the country, away from the madness, I could see that Mummy was finding it hard to talk about my plans for my new life. I had a vocation which she realised was difficult to argue

against. No one could deal with me, far less understand why I had made the decision. My sisters, as might be expected, all said in unison: 'You'll be back in six weeks.'

In the heat of Spain, its blue, untroubled skies allowed me to think more clearly and take stock of the gigantic leap Shirley was preparing to make. I had finally grown up. There was no one who could dictate to me anymore, what I was to do or why I was to do it. Each element of my lost life was analysed. There was my teaching career, which I loved. This could, and would continue in the convent. After all, the Catholic Church, as most other faith schools, led the country in the quality of their teaching (and still do). I would never have children of my own but I would have a hundred others to look after and bring on in their lives. I would not have Jeremy but I would have answered my vocation which, I now understood only too well, had been alongside me since I had been able to sense, and feel and think. So, I became an assistant teacher in order to move forward to the next stage in my life, to understand what it was to become a Catholic. These weighty matters were reviewed, dissected and put back again carefully as they were to be the cornerstones of my future life.

I lay on the sand of what would one day be Torremolinos beach, my heels rising and falling in the shallows. A phrase kept circulating in my head to counter all my positive arguments: I was being tested again. It was a frightening thought for it could have been true for all I knew.

Am I mad? Am I going mad? Was all of this chaos a figment of my imagination? As if senile dementia had come upon me early in life? Perhaps I was already in an asylum with my fragile mind believing

I was being lapped by a placid sea? Did I just imagine I had written those words on the notepaper? And anyway, what were those chairs all about? We had no need for dining chairs.

There was, I decided, no real gravity to me and God was all there was to prop me up and give me some sort of depth of character. I repeated my earlier mantra: I'm just an entertainer, a lightweight with no substance. Why on God's earth does He want me? How could I lead the life of a nun, having had twenty hedonistic years of life with little thought of my fellow Christians in the intervening years?

To underscore the extreme moods assailing me, and in sharp contrast to my brittle mood on the beach, there now came a sense of being on the brink of something quite wonderful. Jeremy rang: he wanted me to know he believed I had found my vocation in life. Having expected a backlash, he could not have been blamed if he had struck out blindly at me, but he had a much better understanding of the primacy of God.

His message to me was simple: 'God has said to me that you are going to be a nun. He is going to look after you.' And, shatteringly, he went on: 'I'm thinking of becoming a Catholic, it is the only way I can stay with you.' Not long after that conversation he let me know that he had indeed converted to Catholicism just as he had planned.

My body trembled. There was a terrible, terrible loneliness in his declaration. It was as if my father's pit props in India had been knocked aside by my own haste to seek out this new life, and Jeremy's own particular roof had come crashing down. From then on, after he became a Catholic, he remained with the vernacular,

the old Latin texts, refusing to move on with the rest of the world into English verses. He was fighting for some sort of recognition in what he was doing. At this stage nothing made sense save for the message I was called to God. He never disputed it, but at the same time he found himself a lost soul seeking an anchor and, perhaps, he also was going through this stage of '*Am I going mad?*

For me, as the world whirled by and spun on into the darkness of space, that February day in 1952 remains inexpressible. There were no more words I could find. I cannot explain it; I cannot believe I could have had a breakdown due to the pressures brought on me because of the forthcoming wedding. But I could not remember why I had been so intent on bidding for those dining chairs at the auction house. I can hardly recall where we were to have lived once we were married, for we had no house and no plans to buy one. The only logic which I could accept was that a strategy for my future had been mapped out on 9 July 1931 in the Grace Dieu hospital, which culminated in my absolute need to go to that auction house twenty years later. I never needed dining chairs – we didn't have a dining room – but I *did* have to write a letter. The chairs, therefore, were simply a mechanism to make me pen the letter. Nothing else makes sense.

I began to justify, if somewhat foolishly, the whole rationale. We had indeed been an item, unofficially engaged, but there were no announcements in the newspapers, no photographs in *Country Life*, not even a ring to flash secretly to my friends. Jeremy had not got down on one knee, holding aloft a small black jewel box, lid open, and said quietly, 'Bunny, will you marry me?' It was just taken in our circle of friends that I was to be married on

3 October 1952, and only on that day because it was St Thérèse's Feast Day and thus I would never forget my wedding anniversary in the future.

My outlook on life was changing as I grasped the fact that on my way, I would now always be accompanied by God. It concerned my mother who, of course, had not changed her own beliefs, remaining steadfastly a Low Church Anglican, but nonetheless she decided to take me off to meet some priests to shed some light on the whole matter. Not Church of England priests, as well she might have done in the past, but real Roman Catholic ones. It showed her love for me in a most particular way.

As we met, one Jesuit priest turned rather magisterially to Mummy, having listened carefully to her arguments before pronouncing, 'Shirley is very wilful and very self-centred.' As you can imagine this went down like a lead balloon, directed as it was towards a highly protective mother. Her eyes glittered. She might not outwardly appear to love her offspring in the manner many parents demonstrate today, but when touched on the raw she would fight to redress the balance. Mother did not like this at all. The priest, however, ignored the brimstone in her eyes and continued, 'They won't keep her if she hasn't a vocation, of that I am sure.'

This second judgement calmed my mother; this was more what she wanted to hear. It was a relief, I suppose, because he was implying I did not have a hope of getting past postulancy to become a novice, even if I reached the starting post. Shirley was evidently not going to make the grade, with or without a good upbringing.

To become a nun you first have to be tested. I felt I was already a seasoned applicant, under a white-hot fire, but if I was to progress into the Order I had first to become a postulant. This was an assessment, a study, with me under the microscope, to be watched to see if the strength of my early resolve would continue, that this was not just a flash in the pan as Didi was apt to believe. The review would last perhaps six months. So many friends, knowing me, believed I would be back on my horse in a few short weeks – more sober, no doubt, and with a more serious attitude to life, but returned to the world I understood.

'It was a nice idea,' they might say, 'but back she will come.' And I recalled my sisters' comments: 'You'll be back in six weeks.'

Just *six weeks*, not even months!

If we passed through this candidature and, depending on the postulant's individual situation, we would be ready to be *clothed*. A curious term, it refers to the fact one puts on the familiar habit, cap and veil, the time when you look like a nun to the person in the street, even if your inner thoughts altered a year earlier. You are accepted and trusted to enter into the period of training ending eight years later when you take your final vows.

To show you how far I had to go in my mental approach to becoming a nun I made a very silly approach to it all: vain, I knew, but I had to know what I would look like as a nun. I had yet to lose this conceit, which at the time meant my appearance mattered to me in front of others. My fashionable dresses, the straightness of the seams in my nylons, my hair, were all important; they had to be right. I imagined, in my calculating mind, Ingrid Bergman as Sister Mary Benedict had nothing on me. I'm ashamed to admit

it today but there it was. In my bedroom I wound a white towel around my head and putting on a soupy face, I stood in front of a mirror with a lighted candle in my hand – for goodness' sake – and stared at the reflected image… of an iced bun.

It would have been fun to have had my siblings with me for we would have collapsed laughing as we had always done in the past. They would have giggled at Darling looking like a cross between a scone with clotted cream on top and a panda bear. Eventually, I took off the towel and blew out the candle, very aware of the fact my first venture into my brave new world was turning out somewhat differently to what I had imagined.

There was some sense behind my apparent inanity. The Congregation of Jesus (C.J.), founded by Mary Ward in 1609, was originally known as the Institute of the Blessed Virgin Mary (IBVM). So when I joined we were to become IBVMs – quite a mouthful. Later, we became C.J.s – in 2003, in fact, so quite recently – and I was able to add C.J. after my name, though this is not a title as a doctor would add, but an indication of the Order to which I would belong. Our Order, the Congregation of Jesus, required their nuns to wear a habit, with a cap and a veil, not a wimple or coif, the familiar image of the nun to the person in the street.

As I waited out my time to becoming a postulant, I little realised or understood the enormous yet necessary changes which would sweep through our faith with the coming of Vatican II in 1965.

*

Between 4 February and the following September when it was arranged for me to enter the IBVM, having been a Roman Catholic for two years (a statutory requirement of the Order), I was determined to continue my life as it had always been. Like that fledgling on the edge of the nest, I knew one day I would have to take off and fly, but for the next few months I would remain surrounded by warm feathers and an adoring mother.

I bought a gorgeous dress for parties, knowing full well I would never wear it out or that it could never fall out of fashion. I would have to give it away to one of my sisters once I entered St Mary's in Ascot. It was a feeling in the pit of my stomach of intense loss mixed with a deep penetrating wonderment of how that particular day would be tackled, when I would have to say goodbye to everything I knew. It was not just fashionable dresses and nylons I would lose; it would be the ability to leave the house on a whim, to have tea with friends or drinks in the evening. I would miss the sudden desire to saddle up my horse at a moment's thought and spend an entire morning riding until hunger would bring me back to the kitchen door. I had no routine, as I would have in the future; I would not be able to open my mouth except at special times of the day. That would be the difficult one. I would not be able to talk to any of my sisters about the issues and problems arising in my life, or to know Mummy was there to introduce me to 'such a nice boy, Darling'.

Like a rush of wind past your ear, gone almost before you can register its force, it was time for me to go. Perhaps I should write, time for me to *start*, to begin the vocation chosen for

me, albeit with my own free consent. Gone would be my lovely home, my ponies, my stables and rabbits. Gone would be Jeremy and the life I might have had with him, but despite all this it's important to stress I was a most willing and eager student, impatient for the future to arrive at my door. I was not being dragged to my chosen life, but it was sad all the same to say goodbye to so many familiar things.

Just as the wind sped past, Thursday, 4 September 1952 arrived – a cool pre-dawn with the promise of a fine day. Jeremy had insisted, against his parents' wishes, to drive me to the convent. It had been very difficult because his father had asked me to write to Jeremy saying I could not see him on his return from Rhodesia on 4 September, as I would already be at St Mary's Convent in Ascot. But Jeremy saw through the words to the duress under which they had been written, and insisted he would be the only one to pass me on to my chosen life.

'I am giving you to God, no one else is going to do this,' he said calmly, yet with considerable determination. He saw it, I think, as an almost sacred act, where I was the most precious thing he could give away.

It meant, of course, amazingly, that he was prepared to fly 5,000 miles just to see I was safely delivered to St Mary's. In those days flights were few and far between Salisbury (Harare) and London, and he could only make 4 September, hence Pafir's request to ensure our paths would not cross in England. The normal entry date at Ascot was to have been the twelfth, so to change it back when Jeremy insisted it was to be him who took me gave me some anxious moments. I had to speak to a

nun about the mix-up and was spoken to by a rather unhelpful member of the community.

'You'll never come if you don't come when you are told,' she replied to my request.

Crestfallen, I tackled Reverend Mother, my Superior-to-be, with the same problem. Would she bend to my early request?

What a darling she was; she readily agreed. 'You come when you want, Shirley. September the fourth will do for us.'

Astonishingly for those days, Jeremy had arranged by cable from Rhodesia for a driver to pick me up in his Lagonda, currently kept in his garage while he was overseas. I was staying in London at the Ladies Carlton Club the night before so I would be ready for the early call. There came a soft knock on the door from the night porter so as not to wake anyone else. It was four o'clock in the morning. I got into the back of the car and had a rug wrapped around my legs by the chauffeur before the man climbed in himself and set off for Northolt. Jeremy was due to fly in, aboard a Comet from Rhodesia.

The beautiful, most modern jet liner in the world landed with a roar of reverse thrust to its engines and in no time at all he was standing in front of me. We kissed, a bit shyly, not even sure whether we should be doing it, then to break the moment I opened my mouth as usual. I was so insecure in my mind as to what to say or do.

'I'm starving, let's get some breakfast.'

As I spoke, my arms stood abandoned by my sides, hands sticking up as if I were a potter about to throw some clay on his wheel.

Jeremy saved the day: 'There's nothing here, let's drive into London.'

In those days I could not have a man inside my club even just for breakfast and Jeremy's club certainly would not permit women to enter his!

London's Northolt Airport was not quite the same in the days before it became Heathrow Airport a few years later, with its malls and restaurants. And there was not a great deal of time. Minutes, seconds, were ticking by and I wanted to be there in the car sharing every last one. Realising the need to be alone, Jeremy told the driver to go home and that he would drive; we needed this smallest amount of time left to us without being overheard by an incredulous driver.

And so we sat as close as we could get in the front seats, aware of the tumultuous feelings flooding the interior, as we drove through the quiet London streets breaking into a dawn, until we found a Lyons Corner House open for breakfast. The enormous spaces in the restaurant might have made us appear lost at that time, but there was a cheerful bustle of early-morning workers seeking a cup of coffee before the start of the day. We built our own mental wall, wrapping us in a tight embrace and curling around our table as we talked of nothing and everything, of Rhodesia and my family, of words simply added to put off the inevitability. It was too difficult to speak of the future in any sense, for either of us, and it would have been a pointless exercise anyway. Eventually, as if it was a scene from *Brief Encounter* without the steam, we had to leave. Before we reached St Mary's Convent Jeremy pulled off the road by a small copse. The two of

us walked away, my little bag clutched in my hand, into a wood, all the while wondering what any passers-by would think as they saw us entering the trees.

It was, of course, to allow me to take off my clothes and dress myself in my new black serge dress. This was not a habit but a copy of a Hattie Simmons from New York, quite smart, though I found out quickly the material was totally unsuitable for my new line of work. In my very small mirror I looked no better than the time in my bedroom and I still did not have my veil, but I had to get used to it for it would be my daily clothing from this day on until I left my postulancy, when I would exchange one black dress for another.

I checked to see my hair was brushed and Jeremey wiped my face and removed any trace of lipstick and make-up for me. Again I stared hard, acceptance giving me a slight shiver down my shoulder blades: this was how I would look, forever, the same face within the same clothes, only the skin would pucker and wrinkle beneath an immaculate cap and veil. My eyes would become rheumy, so I might have to wear round-lensed spectacles with a cheap frame because I could not afford, nor would it be deemed suitable, to wear a pair of designer-labelled frames. They could not be brought into the convent, I'm sure. I carried a new black mackintosh but it was such a bad fit, it was given to the nun who looked after the chickens almost as soon as I was installed inside.

My hands were shaking, my heart banging around so much I believed it could have led to a heart attack, but I forced my thoughts forward, blinkered so they would alight only on the

future. Stronger, I climbed back in the car as Jeremy took my insignificant – and now obsolete – case and placed it in the boot. The tyres crunched on the drive, and the chapel with its semicircular rounded east end in red brick reared up in front of us. My tongue was glued to the roof of my mouth.

'I'll come with you to the door,' Jeremy managed to say.

We walked together up to the main door a few inches apart, not a word between us, our heads staring straight at the door. The buildings were silent as the grave and there was no sign of movement as I rang the bell.

After a long wait the door opened just a few inches. I was about to announce my name but the Sister caught sight of Jeremy and, giving a slight exclamation, closed it again quickly in our faces. She obviously reconsidered her action, having seen a fully dressed postulant in front of her, despite there being a man by her side. The door reopened and with a gesture I alone was told to enter. Nothing was spoken.

All at once I was leaving. No time for a last squeeze of a hand, no comforting phrase uttered like 'Take care, Bunny'. Out of the corner of my eye I saw him simply doff his hat and turn away.

I walked into the building, never daring to look back.

PART TWO

POVERTY, CHASTITY AND OBEDIENCE

7

Ascot – I Lose a Life to Gain a Life

A day in my life as a postulant at St Mary's, Ascot, in 1952:

0540 Rise
0615 Meditation
0645 First mass
0730 Breakfast
0800 Second mass. Office
0900 Manual work. Helping in the kitchen, laundry, refectory, cleaning, box room – e.g. sorting clothes belonging to children
1030 Elevenses
1100 Manual work
1215 Examen
1230 Lunch. We were able to talk and took it in turns to wait

1315 Midday office

1330 Wash up lunch in two galvanised tubs

1400 Recreation together. Walk or remove, perhaps, dead heads from Rhododendrons

1440 Spiritual reading, followed by more manual work

1600 Tea. Clear and lay up for supper

1730 Second meditation

1800 Instruction

1830 Prayers in common, followed by evening office

1900 Supper in silence with reading from the Martyrology, followed by a spiritual book, usually a good biography

1930 Wash up supper

2000 Recreation together in Noviciate Room

2100 Night prayers and evening examen

2130 Go to bed

2200 Usually asleep!

Examen is at 12.15 p.m. and lasts for fifteen minutes. It is also held in the evening. This is where all the nuns meet in the chapel to reflect on where God has been in their lives during the past few hours and to find out where one has departed from the correct path. It was, during those times in the fifties, a very important part of our day which was not to be missed. This has now gone, like so much else, leaving it to the individual's conscience to examine their life.

Office – Divine office means certain prayers are to be recited at fixed hours of the day by a priest, religious or clerics and in

general by all those obliged by their vocation to fulfil this duty. Divine Office consists of three books that set out for each day, three times a day, the recitation of certain prayers.

Martyrology – This is a catalogue of martyrs and other saints arranged in calendar order of their anniversaries and feasts, and the appropriate martyr's name is read out during supper, which is held in silence.

*

I had to be at a considerable disadvantage to all of the other postulants, at least from my own personal viewpoint. My vows, following my novitiate (the training period I was to undergo), were to be Poverty, Chastity and Obedience, and although I was not to take my first vows for another two and a half years, I had to bear in mind that my life would be bound by them in the future.

Poverty – I didn't know what that was. At the age of four I had arrived into a world of extreme comfort, never knowing what it was to be hungry or cold or to be without my ponies, my dolls, my nanny or my groom. I was always clean, my clothes well-pressed, so I was always well-dressed. Poverty to the family was placing a penny in the poor box on a Sunday or listening to the wireless discuss the latest problems of trying to save the starving children in Africa. The Depression had slid past the back door to our house, never stopping for a moment; it simply did not exist. It had been too dismal a subject to think about.

Chastity – I had always been in love with one boy or another. As I grew up I fell into a mad world of parties and dances, where money gave us a sense of being able to achieve anything we

wished, that we were above the ordinary everyday rules we might otherwise have had to live by. Chastity is one of those easily understood words; there is no misunderstanding the term. To be chaste, to have chastity, is to be shown a mark of respect. Some postulants realise they will never achieve this supreme level of purity. Our lives at Sibton and later at Ringleton had always paid lip service to the word during regular sermons, reported to me by my mother, which overused the theme on countless occasions on Sundays. It was a useful subject for the Vicar, writing up his sermon on a Thursday afternoon, to put forward, a moral filler. This enabled the good man to lean over his pulpit and gaze down on the Sibton sisters as if there were no other people in the church, as if we were the only unchaste women in Kent.

Chastity means sexual purity; for those with a religious profession it also means celibacy. It was, however else I looked at it, a daunting idea that having clearly made up my mind on what I wanted to do and be, I had, nonetheless, to remain sexually pure for the rest of my life. There is a temptation to *try it*, to *live it*, and the postulant will have no knowledge on arrival at the convent whether she can withstand the onslaught such pressures entail. There is a very deep chasm bridged by a slender rope bridge. It sways in the slightest gust of wind and bends down towards the powerful river below as it accepts the weight placed upon it. Postulancy sets one thinking very hard from the moment of entry whether or not the mind is strong enough, and will remain as resilient for one's entire life.

Obedience. Now there's a good one to end with, a word I'd had difficulty complying with at all times in my previous

life, with the exception of my mother. Even with her, as soon as the door closed behind her latest ruling, I would forget the imperative laid down upon me, and to the world in general, I would appear disobedient. I never felt I was being insubordinate and I would never have dreamed of hurting Mummy or any of the rest of the family who, with hindsight, had had to put up with a dreadful sense of loss after my father died. While out for a ride on Whisky on a beautiful summer's day I would forget what she had said, carefully navigating around her words, thus in my mind complying with her wishes yet exercising my right to try something new. I had no desire to be disobedient and certainly no desire to go against Mother's wishes, but there were so many exciting things to do and to see. Somehow the promise to be back, washed and changed ready to meet the Vicar for afternoon tea would often go by the wayside.

Obedience also means keeping your mouth shut – politely, of course – much more often than I was able to do. Sister Cecilia Marshall, our Provincial Superior (the Sister in charge of a region or territory) at the time, once said of me, 'Sister Agatha could never put a sock in it', and most regretfully, this was quite true. Without that oh-so-valuable sock, I have run into a lot of trouble in my life. I never mean to be a worry to anyone; it is just that my voice gets carried away on a vision each time it starts up.

And all this was just for starters. Reviewing the daily worksheet, the sense of chastity and obedience were that much easier to follow because, by the end of the day, *any* day for that matter, we cried ourselves to sleep through sheer exhaustion. It allowed little in the way of unchaste thoughts to creep between the pillows

and into my head, or disobedience just to make a point. Poverty was much easier, surprisingly, once I had arrived at Ascot with my few belongings; it was as if my mind had said, I don't need anything else in life, I can get by easily without all the trappings of Sibton.

I wished for nothing else.

*

The complexity of coming to terms with my preparation as a novitiate was only one of the dozens of uncertainties assailing my wits as the big wooden door closed behind me. The nun held up a finger to her lips to ensure I did not speak. It was so quiet I could hear the burble of the Lagonda's exhaust as it went back down the drive, cutting off my last lifeline.

Why was it so quiet?

I was led down to my cell, not a happy phrase to you, which I was to share with a more experienced novice, Sister Martin. Despite nicknames not being permitted in our lives, it didn't take me long to re-christen her 'Aunt Marts', the first of several other changes we made to the postulants' names.

Entering the cell, two beds confronted me on a bare floor, and a small marble-topped cabinet to keep my underclothes, including a chemise under which I wore a pair of calico drawers; there was also a hanger for my two dresses and a picture of Christ on the wall. No personal effects were allowed – no teddy bear at the end of the bed, no doll sitting on my pillow to welcome me back from mass. There was a jug and a bowl for washing, but the water wasn't even lukewarm and ice would form on the surface

when it was very cold during wintertime. The sheets I had sent in earlier were not considered suitable for a postulant and had gone to Mother Cecilia, leaving me with much smaller ones which did not tuck in properly, much to my chagrin. On top of these were Army blankets of the woolly kind. Nothing much else, not even dust, for everywhere was spotless.

My new room-mate (that doesn't sound right, but you know what I mean) communicated in a series of gestures and whispered asides that the convent was in the middle of an eight-day retreat when nobody talked at any time. Had I arrived on the date planned for me, the retreat would have already ended and understanding what was needed of me would have been somewhat easier, for the nuns would have been able to talk to me in the recreation periods. These periods lasted for forty minutes, sandwiched tightly between washing-up lunch and a spiritual reading. For someone as garrulous as me, the whole basis of not talking except at specific times was novel, not to say challenging. I found, in the first few hours, my mouth opening involuntarily – my idea of a guppy in an indoor aquarium tank. My rounded mouth would collapse, usually brought on by a stern eyebrow cocked in my direction. I couldn't even say I'm sorry – for not talking – or rather, sorry for not being able to say sorry for being about to speak, but stopping just in time! It was to be, as the media love to headline, *a steep learning curve*.

That afternoon I came face-to-face with an old London friend, Ann, who had preceded me into the convent. She had always been full of fun and I wondered how she was able to cope with a full-blooded retreat. And she could, proving herself absolutely

worthy of the challenge, but it did not mean she – and me, for that matter – could not have some fun in the meanwhile. By 'fun' I mean taking the stiffness out of the rulebook so although we would not break the rules, we could bend around them to make life a little easier. Flexible friends!

I have explained at the time of my arrival at Ascot, my hair had always been dead straight, not a curl or a wave in sight. For some inexplicable reason I had made the decision to have my hair tight-permed with curls on my forehead, which could then poke out from my veil. I should further explain my veil had been washed in water with a small drop of glue added so it would stand out as if it were a ship in full sail. I think a little too much glue had been mixed for this first occasion. When Ann first saw me, I think it was during tea-time, I began to understand why Jeremy had thrown me such a quizzical arch of one eyebrow in the woods earlier that day, as he'd studied my hair for the first time properly since landing in London.

Ann took one glance at me. It didn't need much studying: tight, snug curls like worm casts and a veil looking as if it were a schooner bearing up to the wind. Her nose twitched, just the once, before she had to turn away quickly so her eyes could study an interesting joint between two blocks of ashlar stone, disowning my own eyes which had sought her out. And then, appallingly, my own nose twitched, without any help from me at all. There was nothing I could do about it, it just happened. To alleviate the problem which had now drifted – well, 'drifted' is the wrong word on reflection, 'tumbled into crisis mode' was better – I needed to raise my face to Heaven and pray fervently that I

would not laugh out loud. After all, that was what I was there for – not to laugh out loud at tea, but to raise my face to Heaven. I was simply terrified my life at Ascot could be terminated in less than twenty-four hours of arrival. How my sisters would have crowed – 'We won the bet!' – and in much less than six weeks.

I concentrated on the dark wood of the beams above as my stomach vibrated in hysterics, but eventually forced my face into an angelic smile and looked past Ann as if she had been an alabaster cherub.

Exhausted, with a joint dose of stress and mirth liberally added to NGS (New Girl Syndrome), I walked back to my cell with Sister Katherine, another postulant, and on the way saw a sink fastened to the wall in the corridor. A prominent notice above the basin read: 'This sink is not a sink'. We both collapsed laughing, quite unable to fathom the instruction out. If it was not a sink then it had to be a useful shelf for worn-out shoes – there were plenty of those in the convent – or torn habits, caps, veils splashed with gravy, or simply something to make us change direction as we walked to our cells. Perhaps it was there to make us think, like a piece of modern art where one has to ponder the artist's creation for some time before the idea behind the thinking behind the paint becomes clear? In fact it was there for us to draw water for washing, but the sink had little or no outlet worth having. Hence the problem. Why it had been put there originally without an outlet was unknown. The community did not use it for anything else, bypassing it on the way without a thought as to its mysterious message. We thus headed for the next duty in the daily programme. The sink remained there, enigmatic, remote; a

sink that was not a sink, yet in its own way a meeting point for discussion for us postulants.

That night, I lay in the darkness, the contrasts with my past life so apparent, alone or almost but for Sister Martin, a million miles from home. I knew beyond a shadow of a doubt I had made the right move for I was no longer on my own: He was in the tiny room with me, His presence as close to me as if He were sitting in the chair. I never questioned His rightness to be there.

And so I slept.

*

Ascot is one of those wonderful places that makes you believe you really have arrived home even as you proceed up the imposing drive. Tall pines frame the playing fields, the buildings are in brick running up into dormers, melding with the countryside. On arrival you feel that you cannot fail to be happy here.

You will find this extraordinary – a silly fool, you will say – but I felt clueless when I arrived at the convent for I had no idea how a nunnery operated and I have to admit, this included not knowing how to pray properly. So I developed a technique whereby as we sat in a line of three black-dressed postulants looking for all the world like a family of crows staring down at a flattened piece of roadkill, I would try and breathe at the same rate as the rest. This would last for half an hour in the kneeling position so I could get the hang of it. There was no other advice or help I could seek. For all of my life as a Church of England parishioner how I was to pray had never entered my mind. Pressing up against me either side would be a Sister in deep devotion while I would be more

interested in who was on the opposite side of the aisle. Looking through steepled fingers – with a useful gap – was natural, but I felt this could not be done in the silence of Ascot's chapel and a whole number of nuns watching my early moves. So I breathed carefully and waited and watched my fellow nuns to see just how they came to terms with the service.

I found I had one advantage which, if I was careful, I could play to an audience. You will recall I liked to act, as did the whole family. As I had been required to read something from the scriptures to my mother every night, I had become, unsurprisingly, somewhat knowledgeable on such weighty matters. It was thus quite easy to contradict a learned nun from time to time – not too often – and advise her she was incorrect on such and such a thesis because 'as you will remember Sister, St Paul did say in…' and on I would prattle. All this was done with movements of my arms and stage presence. I was so ghastly then, manipulative and quite unworthy of the office I sought, but it was God who had called this silly girl to his mass and I had only to follow; I had no option. I was under a focus, a spotlight on my soul throughout my waking days – a prospect I could never have dreamed of a few years earlier.

During the afternoon's 'recreation', as it was termed, we might go for a walk if the weather was nice. Sister Barbara, who had a voice like a nightingale, would tell ghost stories and Sister Bernadette was who we described as a 'safe pair of hands'. Once for a penance in Lent, I made up my mind to spend the recreation break with her, so I could get to know her better. We chatted away on the state of the leaves that year and the signs of squirrels collecting in the fields until Sister Bernadette leaned into me at

one point just as I was gossiping away non-stop. She withdrew a couple of feet before politely turning to face me directly, her face peering out from her veil: 'You shouldn't always walk with me as others might think you are too fond of me!'

So much for my Lenten walk of goodwill. I drifted off to join the rest of the group, leaving Sister Bernadette to her own thoughts.

Surprisingly, or should I say, happily, there was an immense joy in the learning. I might well laugh at life a trifle more than some of my fellow nuns, smile a bit too much at the wrong times, be a bit too loud, and I was, I must admit, described as more of a menace than the other eighteen in the novitiate (hopefully not all together), but I did manage to form a strong bond with my Novice Mistress, Sister Ancilla, a much-loved sister who was an important part of my daily routine. She would smile along with me before suggesting I declare this or that demeanour to the priest at Sunday's Confession. One of those wonderful people who could ensure we were listening to her when it was important, she would study our bowed shoulders and shake her head in wonderment. 'Live! Be alive, enjoy life, and smile at the world,' she would say to us. Sometimes, if we did not react quickly enough for her, she might demonstrate what she meant by leaping onto a refectory table to do a sword dance for us, much to our delight at the break in the regimen of the day.

While life began to be very enjoyable, there arose a singular problem, one that I would never have thought about before entering the community. It was to do with Confession, quite an important part of our week. Living as we did, cloistered, separated

from the real world, where any number of sins might arise on a daily basis, here there was really very little to confess. While at Sibton, I could have filled a priest's day with my wrongdoings. Here, no lascivious thoughts had crossed my mind in the last seven days for we worked until late at night before dropping into a dreamless sleep. I harboured no bad opinions of anyone else for I wanted to make friends, if only so they could guide me through this daily maze. I ate everything up because I was always hungry. So, empty of any valid point, I would enter the Confessional to explain I only had one thing (again) to tell the priest.

'And what is that?' he would enquire (again), yet in a kindly way.

'The only thing I can think of, Father, is I appear to disrupt the day by laughing,' to which the priest himself would laugh out loud. Here was a human man in the real sense of being human, who warmed my heart.

I learned too from a friendly nun, Katherine, of the rules about talking, or rather *not* talking. Because one did not have to say how many times one had transgressed the no-speaking rule in a week, it had been calculated by the postulants (us) that by making sure we spoke out on a Monday, we could then speak all week, albeit in whispers. Then we would own up on Friday, 'having spoken out aloud at the wrong time'.

Yet, as so often in the contrariness of my nature, when we were finally on a full retreat, I found I had no desire to speak. It was as if something inside of me commanded that Sister Agatha needed to remain silent and I was happy to comply. When not in a retreat, we were able to speak during recreation time, though

usually we didn't reminisce on the past. Our other life was now so distant it seemed as if it had all been a daydream.

Katherine, now established as a close companion, had been made aware of my life with Jeremy and inevitably, in such a confined life where we lived right on top of each other, the news eventually seeped out. How many other nuns, I wondered, had experienced similar ordeals which they had had to overcome before arriving on the doorstep of Ascot?

Learning became more thoughtful, deeper and more complex. I became a sponge, soaking up the mysteries of my calling. We were instructed in Ignatian prayer, with Justice, Truth and Humility to reflect upon. It meant we had to kneel to proclaim our faults. Based on my previous life I could have proclaimed for hours if necessary, but in the end we would have had to go to bed. Ignatian teaching was a strong and powerful force, I learned, and found I was in sympathy with the ideals, so it was never a problem for me to understand and to agree with its ethics. It was a good, symbiotic relationship.

The sheer growing enjoyment of my life began to build block-on-block with this solemn and fervent side to our instruction. Contrary to my earlier belief I might come into conflict with my earlier self, that I would be bored and give it all up as a failed event, I found every day my decision to change, to move to a new existence, was increasingly fulfilled with intense satisfaction. It reconfirmed my impression I had been chosen with a part to play in the great plan, albeit, I was fast coming to the realisation, a very small part, like a walk-on soldier in a Shakespearean play.

The convent was integrally linked to the school, an

independent institute. After the war the community had gone through a testing time reacting to the 1944 Education Act, which required all boys and girls to remain in education until they were fifteen years old. When I arrived, the school was already full to overflowing and an ex-Army hut was purchased for £595, dismantled, moved and reconstructed next to St Francis's church. Four years later, we would need a second. Each time we added a building we needed paths and water and electricity, apart from heating of some kind for the children, the extra books and paper, pens, desks and chairs. It all had to be planned.

While this constant state of motion was continuing around me I found a month had gone past in the bat of an eyelid. I had slipped into the routine which governed every waking moment of my life. There wasn't a moment in the day that was not regulated in some way. It was the complete antithesis of my previous life.

St Therese's Feast Day, 3 October, would not have been any different to any other October day except it was to have been the day I was to be married. To my surprise my heart did not do a wobble, for my mind was becoming more resolved with each day that passed. I have to admit, however, to pondering on a what-if basis of how it might have gone, whether my sisters would have decked themselves out, going right over the top with their fashionable dresses, whether Mother would have fussed over my veil (*another* sort of veil) when it flew in my face in the wind, and if Jeremy might have been facing back up the aisle as I approached. Such a gesture would have rounded the service off nicely.

I slowly became aware Jeremy had begun to call every month at the convent to ask after my happiness. A note would be relayed

to me later in the day of his enquiry by Sister Ancilla, and I would simply acknowledge the message with a slight nod of my head and a half-smile to say I understood. I cannot but wonder if his eyes would have strayed from side to side as he peered through the main doorway in case he saw me walking to mass.

The strength of his feelings for me can only be judged by the fact he continued to call month after month, seeing the seasons fall away as I progressed towards my own chosen way of life. It began to dawn on him that I had found my vocation, and I was not going to change. Time to draw a line under what had been a truly wonderful part of his life; it was over. What was to help him was his sense of humour, which rarely, if ever, left him. There were still parties to attend, dressed to the nines in whatever outrageous costume he could find. There were people to tease and to enjoy a joke with. Then, and only then, did he realise he had experienced something good in his life, that he had not made a mistake by involving himself with me but that the time had come to start again and find a loving wife. It had been good but it was over.

I returned to my cell on that October day, having glanced outside to realise it would have been a nice day for the wedding. Ann gave me a squeeze of the hand to acknowledge the fact and my life rolled onwards.

*

To some of my Sisters, each day was brightened considerably by the advent of mealtimes. There were, astonishingly, five meals a day when the whole community came together to eat. At 7.30 in the morning we would breakfast on All-Bran or some such

cereal designed to *do us good*. Some days we had what was called a 'hot-fork breakfast' (a cooked meal), but this was not on the menu all the time. At 10.30 we stopped for elevenses – a curious word, don't you think, especially at ten-thirty in the morning? And why did we stop before eleven? But this period of downed tools brought, delight of delights, beef dripping on bread! *Woman's Own* magazine would be appalled today to think we ladies would wolf this basic food down with all its calories, but as we were burning up a whopping 3,000 of them each day, the dripping kept us in trim. Today, dripping has gone the full circle and some food gurus say it's fine to eat as part of a calorie-controlled diet and is healthier than butter. But for us it was just plain delicious and, two hours later, having worked off the layer of beef lard with another hour or so of manual work, it was time for lunch. This was our main meal of the day, with the kitchen serving up a meat-and-two-veg and a pudding. It was never spectacular but neither was it poor food and I remember I always enjoyed our meals.

Fish, always of course on Fridays, came with an added benefit – would you believe what I am going to say? – of being permitted to use soap flakes (possibly Lux) in the washing-up water to help remove the taste of cod and haddock from the plates. During this meal there would be a reading for about ten minutes, with grace in Latin. Around this, we took it in turns to serve the food.

By four we were quite ready for afternoon tea with bread and jam but no butter as it was still very difficult to get hold of, with the war a lingering memory to remind us we weren't back to pre-war, pre-rationing comforts. This all had to be cleared

away before laying up for supper, the least enjoyable meal for postulants, who were given a concoction bravely labelled 'hot chocolate', though, regretfully, it fell far short of the real thing, having far too much bitter cocoa added.

We, like every child in the land at that time, were not allowed to leave any food on the plate, save for a piece of lamb gristle. It was part of the nation's culture, poles apart from today's wasteful eating. We ensured we would leave nothing because we were a small village in ourselves and in control of our way of living. The convent even had its own Guernsey cows, so fresh milk was on tap, or rather, on *churn*, every day. Attending to the cows required me, one day, to go and collect a new bull called Friendly Boy – funny how names like this remain in your mind half a century after the event. Friendly Boy's byre has now been turned into a music centre, but at the time collecting a big bull that day and walking it back to the convent made me feel like Jack from Beanstalk fame about to swap beans for my cow. He was delivered to the convent safely but no beanstalk arose and no giant rumble in the sky.

These mealtimes occupied quite a considerable proportion of our time throughout the day if you include laying up and washing up. We did set our standards high, making me think of Sibton days and the butler laying up for dinner. We had brought with us damask table napkins, which we kept in cloth bags, each with our own number: mine was 113. The glass and cutlery sparkled, the food was good, and soon I had to wear a black cardigan I had sensibly brought with me in my little case as my expensive black serge dress split under the arms. I had lost a lot

of weight during the ordeal of the break-up with Jeremy, and my new contentment meant it was all being replaced… but this time in all the wrong places.

To deal with all of this food and not being permitted to have expensive toothpaste we were provided with an interesting, to some, mixture of salt and bicarbonate of soda to do the job instead, though visits to the dentist did not appear to be any more frequent than in the other world outside the walls.

The simple entry of 'Manual Work' on our daily timetable was certainly a misdirection or, one should say, a novel view of what the word 'Manual' entailed. There were huge areas both in the school and the convent to clean. By 'cleaning', I mean sparkling clean, which any hospital today would probably kill for. Determined to shine (sorry, another pun), I made up my mind to polish every single brass door knob in the novitiate building with good old Brasso, a small penance of my own creation and to make each handle as good as Wright our butler had achieved at Sibton. Old memories die hard. Eventually, hands blackened, tired out, but triumphant, I turned to see the Novice Mistress staring down at me on my knees, a frown upon her forehead and a finger tapping on the door frame. I gazed up for some reward, knowing it was wrong but, well, it was nice to have one occasionally.

She shook her head: 'Now we shall always have to clean every handle in the building.'

'Ah, yes, I suppose so, Sister.'

Sigh from me, shoulders depressed as far as they would go; longer sigh from the Novice Mistress. I examined my fingernails

carefully, wondering how I would be able to clean them before the evening calls.

To lighten the day a gang of us would steal away and climb up into the attic of the infirmary through a hatch, which we would then drop back in place, as if clearing up after a long day's digging a tunnel in Stalag Luft III. We would whisper, too loudly, exchanging jokes, knowing we were being disobedient and yet believing we weren't doing anything too wrong, nothing that God might take a frown at, even though we knew He could see us bunched up together in a giggling mass in the dark and we hoped He might smile at our silliness. Then we would climb down after calling out 'All clear!' or 'Cavey!' if someone was coming, before going back to our tasks with a secret smile on our faces.

There are two ways of looking at these high jinks and outward expressions of youth. First, we were young, developing our minds as all adolescents must do; we transgressed but in a very small way, and we remained attached to achieving our three vows. The second was that it was a healthy environment we lived in; we were being tested almost every day and we knew that there would be very tough boundaries to cross in the future. The deviations, such as they were, would have been laughed at and accepted as a normal part of growing up had we been living in the other world.

As we grew more knowledgeable, we 'put away childish things' and became more serious and caring for others. It was all part of the learning process as we moved towards being clothed.

8

Clothing the Nun

I was learning, albeit slowly. I had to learn because my education to date had been, to say the least, bitty and old-fashioned, with large chunks missing completely. My future life as a nun meant I had to be properly trained. There was some concern, in some quarters, that I had not reached the standard of education I needed to be able to teach. I had entered the convent with a failed O-level in something and a driving licence was the only other piece of documentation I owned. Roman Catholic schools were some of the best in the country and their reputation needed to be maintained. Hence, Agatha had to be taught subjects her governesses had never considered she would need in the land of privilege and wealth.

At Ascot I had to be sufficiently accomplished in a range of subjects to enable me to pass the entrance exams to be accepted

at college, which included a carefully managed interview. There was a possibility I could carry out a three-year course in domestic science, which would require me to know something also about geography and science, both subjects I had never covered before. Literature was another subject, but this one I loved, and poetry I found magical. Nothing had been decided yet as to what I was to do, and I knew I would have to submit to whatever direction I was to be sent in the future. We forget that in 1952, girls only rarely had the same advantages as boys, so a balance had to be found between what we needed absolutely to know and those subjects which might be nice to have in our heads but were not essential. Girls achieving university places were still talking points in many parts of the UK, notwithstanding it was a continually improving area.

The convent became a wonderful educator for me. Without its guidance I might well not have been accepted at college and thus would never have known the delight of teaching cooking to girls and for them to cook well. A passion was beginning to develop, a passion to teach, knowing that it was wrong to use God's creations badly. Food was to be cooked as well as it could be achieved; God's fruits were not to be spoiled in the making. It made great sense to me.

*

The time it had taken was much shorter than some, longer than others. A decision had been made, approval expressed and passed on to me. I was to become clothed on 26 April 1953, seven months after that door had closed quietly behind me.

CLOTHING THE NUN

To be 'clothed' is our term when we move from being a postulant into a new estate, that of a novice. The ceremony, for that is what it is, dates back to the beginning of the monastic institutions, where clothing brought the postulant together with her family, her friends and the community.

What on earth does it mean? It means that having been assessed, the decision to admit or reject the postulant from moving to the next and higher stage in her life is made by the Provincial Superior and her Council, having consulted with other Sisters. At this time she is presented, clothed in a habit and cap and veil, in front of her blood family and her community family. Before this highly formal ritual, the postulant goes into retreat for eight days, seeing the world outside the convent for the last time.

Invitations are sent out by the Reverend Mother, two new habits are made from the finest of materials, one for Sunday and the other for the working week. We were not supposed to wash these habits despite the hard work we had to do, but of course we did launder them when it was necessary. To protect the habit, I would wear a blue-and-white checked apron, which I made from some spare material; I received the nickname 'peachy' from the schoolchildren because of my pink-and-white complexion! Then came my white cap and black veil; I was transformed. Incidentally, my Order did not wear a wimple or coif; these were for the enclosed Orders.

I made a crass mistake, brought on by a mixture of lack of knowledge about the ceremony and being too proud to ask, when the special habits were delivered to my cell. I had believed 'being clothed' was to be a physical act, as if some nun, or nuns,

dressed me in my habit and cap and veil as some sort of religious act in itself. I hadn't quite worked out how this could happen in front of all the parents and children attending the ceremony but believe it, I did. So I stood half-naked – well, fairly well undressed – waiting for the clothes which were now blessed to be placed over my head. Not a lot happened for a while, so I waited some more. I waited, wondering when they would come, but the mood was eventually broken by the entry of my Novice Mistress, wondering quite what was going on. She took one glance at me, sized up the situation and said, 'For goodness' sake, get dressed, girl!' As I said before, it was a steep learning curve.

But I was not alone. I could hear a slight argument arising in another postulant's cell close to mine, probably brought on by nerves, as she was being clothed. One voice said, 'Don't speak to me like that, I'm a clothed nun.' To which the riposte came fairly soon after from the postulant, I have to assume, 'What do you think I am?' Wedding day nerves, I'm sure. It soon dissipated with the start of the occasion.

And so the twenty-sixth dawned, a beautiful day, which became ridiculously hot for the time of the year at London Airport, where Jeremy and I had last kissed. The day before was a magical day, for two clever men, Francis Crick and James D. Watson, had published their interpretation of the double helix structure of DNA. This was to send all of mankind, believers or not, on a long voyage of discovery, still not ended, into who we were and where we came from. It would challenge us all as the world realised the incalculable benefits which would accrue in the years to come.

The beautiful church of the convent, with its curving beams standing out from the white ceiling reflecting the purity of the occasion, was matched only by the large flower arrangements everywhere made up of white lilies. We waited in high anticipation for the arrival of our families and I immediately recognised Didi's high heels click-clacking over the glowing polish of the floor. I could see she had already stolen a camellia from our garden for her buttonhole. She acknowledged me with a slight wave of her hand. Dear Didi, she hadn't changed a bit, nor did I want her to.

The ceremony was very formal, wonderful in its austere correctness, and I could see many a tear in the eyes of the congregation. It was not an exaggeration to say that to some families it was as if their daughter had died, lost forever from the comfort and familiarity of their past lives. And one could understand why. In an instant held in time, as if in slow motion, I saw the moment when it dawned on my family they were losing me forever, not for an extended holiday, but for all time. I was no longer to be part of my family; no laughs and giggles in the bedrooms as we tried out our hats for a lunchtime 'do'. My sisters would be losing the butt of most of their jokes. I was the baby, so much younger than them. From now on they would not be able to complain about the rabbit droppings in the backyard. Pammy would not be able to throw slippers at me in frequent rages in her bedroom (her tempers were legion). My mother, dear Mummy, would not be able to buy me a new scarf on a whim while out shopping and for them all, horror of horrors, who was going to cook? As the ceremony progressed there were so many changes

being wrought that I could spend a day listing them all. There was not a part of my life that was not to change.

Sadly, they returned to London for their own party, where I was told later they cried into their handkerchiefs at the sadness of knowing I was losing even the name Shirley, if gaining that of Agatha. To them, though, I was to be forever Shirley, or rather, 'Darling'. They simply could not come to terms with the new name. The name Agatha, at least, never changed. Two years later, taking my First vows should have meant being addressed as 'Mother', but a decision of the General Council in the 1950s meant this was not to be. I was never to answer to the title. It was only when I became Superior (in charge) that I was called Reverend Mother, which lasted into the eighties after which even this title was dropped.

And so I returned to my old routine, clothed now in a habit and looking like a nun, determined to work hard to get to college.

*

I am a tactile sort of a person, a touchy-feely nun. A habit (sorry!), I suppose, from sharing with three sisters, though not learned from my mother. She was not a hugger, but everyone else in our family touched and hugged, kissing each cheek as if tomorrow would never come. It was a natural thing to do at Sibton. At Ascot, this simply did not happen of course; it was not part of our life. It was difficult to give a kiss to someone when you didn't even talk to them for a good part of the day. There was, though, one occasion when the barrier broke and it was, I think, for an acceptable reason – and I was *very* stressed at the time.

Friday's fish had not been delivered to the kitchen and I stood with another, older cook and stared at the floor, for although we were quite capable of providing an alternative meal, we could not do so on a Friday. It was fish or nothing; there was no option. We growled quietly in a corner as we studied the clock, with no mobile in those days to call up the van to find out where it was. At the last minute the delivery arrived and I was so relieved, I embraced the other cook, clinging to her for a moment.

'We don't do that here, Sister Agatha,' came the not unkind reply. I checked myself, brushing it off as a foolish lapse, and turned my attention to getting lunch ready for a hungry community and school expecting fish for lunch.

It reminded me at the time of how members of the public are advised on how to shake hands with the Queen and to ensure they do not touch her anywhere else, least of all not to put an arm around her shoulder. I recall the furore when Paul Keating, the Australian Prime Minister, did just that during Her Majesty's 1992 tour of Australia. We simply did not do hugging.

Hugging is a natural expression of fondness, of showing love. It is a form of communication far above today's feeble social contacts. I love to be kissed twice when I meet someone, once on each cheek just as the French do, though not three as the Dutch insist or even Russian men. Then a similar dose of niceness when I say goodbye. For me it is an act of courtesy, an invitation to come back again, but nothing more than that.

There was never a moment, now I was clothed, of doing nothing. It was difficult to slide a piece of paper between the end of one job and the start of the next, so going into retreat

for eight days proved a blessing. We spent the days in silence while we were on our own with our retreat director. There was a concentration of prayer and we spent a minimum of four hours each day with fingers steepled. It is to my eternal regret to admit I would go to sleep at times, brought on by sheer fatigue and, yes, boredom. I told my director this on one retreat and he raised an eyebrow when I mentioned the 'B' word. It was a word he was fairly keen on removing from my repertoire as soon as it was possible. Besides, he could see nothing boring in contemplation. He needed to address the state of affairs which had been imported into our retreat house.

'I want you to go away, Sister Agatha, and pray for an hour on all things you can think of concerning the Good Shepherd.'

I bobbed – we all bobbed everywhere – before bowing my head in deep contemplation. Bobbing, in those early days, was an automatic gesture, made without a thought and it was part of our daily lives. We thought nothing of it, so we bobbed at everyone to make sure we had covered the ritual and then got on with what we were doing. The act of bobbing has now disappeared, along with so many other routines in our lives.

Attending to my instructions, nothing came to mind other than a blank sheet of paper. Then an image appeared in hazy detail, a picture I had had on the wall of my day nursery in Sibton. It was of our Lord, looking soupy in one of those white nightdresses, clutching a lamb. Most, if not all, pictures of Jesus of the Victorian period were of the same ilk and one could admire or replace them with one's own favourite image at will. After an hour I recounted my thoughts, adding silently, 'God preserve

me from all that.' There were many other uplifting religious paintings through the centuries I would rather have on my wall.

The director hummed and hawed in some frustration. 'Sister Agatha, I would like you to go away for another hour and ponder on the same subject. I am sure, in the end, you will find the rightness of things I have asked you to do.'

That made *me* hum and dither. Another hour on the same subject, where I had run out of ideas the first time around. I know, I thought, with some sinful pride, I will pretend to be a fat lamb sitting in the lap of Jesus. No, on second thoughts, perhaps not. The image summoned was not one the director was going to be too happy about.

Another hour trundled by, and almost at the end of the allotted time I had an inspiration. I rose and faced the director with a much more confident smile.

'Well, Sister Agatha, do you have a more improved view of the Good Shepherd? Something deeper, something more meaningful than your earlier attempt?' He could see quite clearly I had gone through some sort of transformation as it must have shown on my face. And now I was ready with my answer.

'Yes,' I replied with gathering sureness in my voice. 'Yes. I asked the Lord, "Will I do?" And He replied to me, "No, Agatha, certainly not." But…' Here, I paused for slight effect, '"but, because the Lord loves you, you'll do."'

The director's nose trembled for a second in time, though he didn't repeat either the hum or the haw. 'Well, Sister Agatha,' he said eventually, 'you can use that persuasion for the rest of your life. It will probably hold you in good stead.'

He passed on to another room and I sat there, realising that He had spoken to me, I hadn't just made something up to get through the hour. As predicted, I have recalled this incident all of my life.

*

I was working, as I told you, on the preparation of my vows: Obedience, Chastity and Poverty. By small degrees I began to understand the great order of things, what it was all about. These Ignatian vows are planned by all recently clothed nuns to be regularly renewed. It is worth taking time out here to tell you about Ignatius as he was the man, born in Castile in 1491, who founded the Society of Jesus, the Jesuits as we know them. Ignatius became the Society's first Superior General. He had discovered in his own life that God was working all around him, that He was there to help. Ignatius went on to help others discover God in their own lives. Out of this simple start the retreat movement was born.

Ignatius was a Spanish knight from a noble Basque family and after being wounded in the Battle of Pamplona at the age of twenty he underwent a spiritual conversion and became a hermit while he formulated the fundamentals of what he later described as 'The Spiritual Exercises'. He studied theology and formed a group binding themselves under the, by now, familiar vows of Poverty, Chastity and Obedience, which hailed from the time of the Desert Fathers. His devotion was characterised by his absolute obedience to the Pope. After his death at the age of sixty-four he was beatified (the stage before sainthood) by Pope Paul V and

then canonised by Pope Gregory XV. He is the foremost patron of soldiers, would you believe?

It is important to make clear that the IBVM as we were then (now the Congregation of Jesus) is an Ignatian Congregation – that is, Apostolic and not Monastic – and thus these vows are interpreted in an apostolic sense rather than the monastic.

*

During the time of postulancy and then into my novitiate I could, if I had been so minded, walk out of the convent on any day of the week, having decided the life was not for me. Had I been mistaken in my vocation it would never have been held against me. Most nuns, especially myself, with a total belief in my vocation, knew after the first year those promises they had made to themselves were as strong then as they had ever been. I did not have to be reminded; it was not difficult to keep my vows.

There was, however, one issue left stranded in my mind, a lost memory of those old days, which refused to be cleansed from my thoughts. Although I knew I had been absolutely right in accepting my calling, there was a single memory so deep-seated I had to acknowledge its constant presence. It should, I suppose, have challenged my responsibilities but, instead, it caused me to turn to verse. I have always loved poetry, some of it astonishingly beautiful, and in this category I include the works of Alice Meynell. There is one poem especially which remains with me forever – it is almost as if Alice wrote this for me in my cell at night. It is called 'Renouncement'.

Renouncement
I must not think of thee; and, tired yet strong
I shun the thought that lurks in all delight –
The thought of thee – and in the blue heaven's height
And in the sweetest passage of a song
Oh, just beyond the fairest thoughts that throng
This breast, the thought of thee awaits, hidden yet bright;
But it must never, never come in sight;
I must stop short of thee the whole day long.
But when sleep comes to close each difficult day,
When night gives pause to the long watch I keep,
And all my bonds I needs must loose apart,
Must doff my will as raiment laid away –
With the first dream that comes with the first sleep
I run, I run, I am gathered to thy heart.

Alice Meynell

I place in bold type the last line. Despite my love of God, my utter belief in the rightness of my actions taken in my, as yet, young life to be a nun, at night I still gathered Jeremy to my heart in my sleep. It never happened when I was awake, but stole over me as I drifted off after a long day. It is simply not possible to remove such a love from one's memories, besides which, what great sin would I commit for recalling those happy days? Surely it cannot be a sin just to love someone even when it cannot be consummated – ever?

The roots were so deep and to pull them out so painful it took me until I was thirty-eight years of age, in 1969, before I was able to sleep without dreaming those thoughts. They had been

my teddy bear at the end of my bed, my Jeremy doll, my nanny. The near presence of Jeremy, reminding me he was still living in the area, for I knew he called each month at the convent door, brought another issue to light. Like London buses, another was right behind the first.

*

It came as another jolt, a blow to the calmness of the life I had adopted. Worry and stress were not issues common to our lives in Ascot even if they did exist from time to time. For stress to push its ugly nose not once but twice so close together in my life was deeply upsetting. I knew that Jeremy had become a Catholic soon after I had entered the Catholic Church, though his family remained staunch members of the Church of England. Now, a year later, out of the blue, I was given the news he was waiting to enter Downside Monastery: Jeremy was to become a Benedictine Monk. His reasons for so doing quickly failed to show up even a trace of a vocation in his plan. It was simply and solely, I am convinced, to 'stay close to me'. For me this was mind-numbing knowledge to accept for it followed on from the earlier time when he had converted to Catholicism, now seemingly for the same reason. He could not, of course, have ever been able to be any closer. Our paths had separated and would never cross again, but it never stopped me from gathering his enormous power to love to my heart each night.

That evening I wept in the chapel; I couldn't help it. The other nuns whispered in my ear, 'Are you alright?' to which I just said, 'Yes.'

They whispered to each other, 'What's wrong with her?' One nun, who knew me better, replied: 'Something to do with J, I expect.'

My head on my pillow, moonlight bars across the bed cover, I repeated:

> But when sleep comes to close each difficult day
> When night gives pause to the long watch

I would close my eyes content in the knowledge that, having known such a love, I would be the better for it than those who could only listen and wonder at the prospect. But there was a second case to argue: throughout my life I would often have to listen to stories of sadness, of lost love and of unrequited love from lay families and individuals. My argument is that I could not only understand people's sorrow when related to me but because of my previous life, I had been chosen because I could understand the intensity which love can bring and the sublime feeling of being loved.

Jeremy's love for a woman had caused him, without a vocation, to try and change his whole life in an act of what I could only think of as blind folly. Frustratingly to him, his own love was unable to complete the cycle of falling in love, engagement, marriage, happy ever after. And, as time advanced, the gap continued to widen as if a steamship was leaving the dockside bound for Australia, never to return. Slowly, he began to understand he might have to find someone else. As God would have it, he did find another woman to love and someone

to provide the sensibility and common sense as well as the love he needed. What was right and good for me to understand was that he found his wife not on a rebound but through his own love seeking out a soulmate of his choosing. That sounds a bit mawkish but it's a fact borne out by his many friends. In the end I went back to my studies and let the other world move on without me.

*

I had moved on to the highly significant stage that is known as the Profession of Temporary Vows at a time which usually lasts a period of six years. Permission to take vows can be for one, two or three years at a time, depending on the individual. This was to be a very important point in my progress on a vocation. Depending upon the length of vows, at first Profession there will be a renewal – or not – when this provisional period has lapsed. The individual applies to the Superior to take or renew vows but the decision to do so lies with the General Superior. Then, professed but before my Final vows, I become a 'Junior'. This was the stage I now entered.

Eventually, after discussion with Mother Cecilia about my forthcoming interview to attend college in London, I found out that the decision on what I was to study was still in the balance. I knew what *I* wanted to do, but there was a small point about my vow of Obedience I had to attend to. So I waited, listening. Possibly my obedience was being tested to the utmost and there was never the chance, in those days, for me to challenge the mission once given.

I now entered Mother Cecilia's office, bobbed and glanced up quickly at her face as I attempted to read the rune stones in her eyes. There was nothing there that could give me the slightest hope of having what I so desperately wanted.

Mother Cecilia studied me back for a moment with a glance over her glasses at my round face and straight hair peeking out as if it were an early morning snail seeing fresh lettuce right ahead. 'Sister Agatha, someone is needed to teach geography. Would you like to take up the subject, learn more about the world and all things within it?'

The phrase, 'Would you like…?', a simple enough request, bore no reflection on its real import. One was *missioned* in life, a suggestion was put forward and one agreed to the proposal. My mind trembled, knowing I must agree, but I wanted to cook.

'I have never learned geography, Reverend Mother. It was not a subject we had to cover when I had governesses, nor subsequently at Miss Faunce's. I know absolutely nothing about the subject.'

Mother Cecilia squinted at me again before adding a half-sigh to the room. But there was also a half-smile on her face; she had been expecting me to open my mouth somewhere along the line. Before she could speak, I added another gem for her to digest: 'The geography teacher went off to war and never came back.'

There came a long suspension of time. Some describe such an interval as a pregnant pause, for some reason. 'Very well, Sister Agatha. It is obviously not to be geography. I think therefore it should be domestic science, "Dom.Si" to you and me.'

I couldn't help it. God had smiled – I was going to be a cook, a *better* cook, and then I could train others to do the same.

Above: A photograph of my parents in the car in Simla. Didi is being held in the back seat by her Ayah.

Below right: The only existing photo I have of the two of my parents together.

Above left: Me at three, before I lost my puppy-fat.

Above right: Jeremy in 1937.

Below: A modern photograph of Sibton Park gardens, which look no less splendid now as they did when I grew up there during the war.

Above left: My mother, Ximena, was always the most beautiful of us all.

Above right: Me at the age of twenty-one. Taken for *Country Life Magazine*.

Below: Me at the Gymkhana in 1947. How I loved to ride.

A lovely, happy photograph of sister Didi's wedding to Geoffrey, although their marriage would be less happy.

THE BAR CONVENT

The Bar Convent in York is the oldest living convent in England, and is run by sisters from the Congregation of Jesus. It was founded in 1686 as a Catholic school for girls by wealthy Catholic landowner Thomas Gascoigne, who bequeathed the sisters £450 after declaring, 'We must have a school for our daughters!'

The only flaw was that the Catholic faith was banned in England at the time and the penalties for breaking this law were severe – in 1646 the head of a priest had been impaled on a spike at Micklegate Bar, close to the chosen spot for the new school. But the sisters persevered and the Bar Convent flourished, surviving angry Protestant mobs even Luftwaffe bombs.

The original house was rebuilt in the eighteenth century, into th fine Georgian structure that has pride of place at the top of Blosso Street. The school closed in the 1980s and became a guest hous and museum, which was recently refurbished. The guest house is now open seven days a week and attracts guests from as a fa afield as China, with rave reviews. The museum, now open ever week day, was replaced with a brand new accessible and interactive exhibition that tells not only the story of the house but of Mary Ward and the movement she founded.

But the heart of the Bar Convent remains the same: the eighteenth-century secret chapel, hidden away beneath a false roof, still reminds of us of the convent's difficult past and the walled garden provides an oasis in the heart of York. The underlying message of welcoming those 'of all faiths and none' is as true today as it ever was.

A Nun's Story